Julia McGuinness is a freelance wri... writes for Redemptorist's 'Sunday I... has produced articles for other publ... *Creative Praying in Groups* (SPCK, 2... both privately and at a National Health Service general practitioners' surgery. Julia is also a qualified Myers-Briggs consultant and has run workshops in secular environments and church settings. She is a Reader at St Thomas' and All Saints', Ellesmere Port with St Lawrence's, Stoak Village, a parish with a varied range of churchmanship across its different services.

MAKING THE MOST OF MIDLIFE

Christian Choices for Change and Growth

Julia McGuinness

First published in Great Britain in 2006

Society for Promoting Christian Knowledge
36 Causton Street
London SW1P 4ST

British Library Cataloguing-in-Publication Data
A catalogue record for this book is available from the British Library

ISBN-13: 978–0–281–05787–0
ISBN-10: 0–281–05787–7

1 3 5 7 9 10 8 6 4 2

Typeset by Graphicraft Ltd, Hong Kong
Printed in Great Britain by Bookmarque Ltd, Croydon, Surrey

Contents

————•◆•————

Preface

'Jesus was never middle-aged!' my 40-something mother once exclaimed in a moment of rarely expressed frustration, to me, her teenage daughter. A relatively new and eager young Christian at the time, I struggled, and failed, to find a fitting response. Now a seasoned midlifer myself, personal experience and heart-to-heart conversations with peers have brought me some understanding of what lay behind her comment, and its memory raises a rueful smile.

Midlife transition raises significant issues in our lives. It cannot be pigeon-holed into one narrow age-bracket: some have felt its rumblings in their thirties; others have found it taking them by storm in their fifties. And while readers going through life-changes at any stage will find some relevant material in this book, a hallmark of midlife transition is that so many concerns and pressures arise at once, and often seemingly out of the blue.

Whatever the Son of God's earthly lifespan, our creator cares about midlife upheaval. Indeed, God himself can become more of a focus for us at midlife than ever before, as personal vulnerability and a search for meaningful values come to the fore.

As with any transition, our response affects the nature of the outcome. The choices we make at midlife can enrich the rest of our lives, if we are willing to embrace the opportunity. It is my hope that in charting the landscape of this unique season, you will be encouraged and enabled to face midlife creatively, and discover that through God's grace, the best can actually start in the middle.

It is important to stress that the names and in many cases significant details of the personal stories featured have been changed to preserve anonymity. An exception to this is the Revd Christine Mullins, whom I was privileged to interview for the *Church Times* during the writing of this book. I am especially grateful for her reflections on the image of the 'walled garden', which have inspired the book's cover design.

Acknowledgements

———•◦•———

'Stop' by Sue Mayfield, on pages 38–9, was composed and performed at the Northern Province Clergy Spouses' Retreat at Scargill House in Yorkshire in 1996. It is reproduced in Chapter 4 with her kind permission.

'Reflections on life's road', in Chapter 8 (page 101), has previously appeared in *Our Hearts Still Sing*, a book of readings and reflections by Peter Millar and Neil Paynter (Wild Goose Publications, 2004).

1

Charting the midlife landscape

Train travelling

My father always chose the train seat facing backwards,
Watching everything that had just passed by:
Imposing buildings shrinking into model villages,
Cows in fields whisked away in mid-graze,
People shrinking into dots on the horizon,
As he viewed the panorama of things past,
Sitting back and at ease.

I always wanted a forward-facing seat,
Straining to see what lay ahead:
Whole communities leaping into life from grey blurs,
Tiny trees shooting up into majestic oaks in a flash,
People hurtling to meet me, new faces forever emerging.
I loved to see the promise of things to come shape into substance,
Sitting on the edge of my seat.

But these days I don't know where to place myself.
The looming landscape has lost its thrill,
I could take my father's seat; it's empty now,
But I'm not ready to watch life drop away into the distance.
So I stand, lurching uncertainly in the carriage,
Sure of nothing,
Except that we will stop at the end of the line.

Julia McGuinness

Mid-life is a time of challenges and crossroads.

Craig Nathanson

The young have aspirations that never come to pass, the old have reminiscences of what never happened. It's only the middle-aged who are really conscious of their limitations.

Saki

Why are you cast down, O my soul,
and why are you disquieted within me?
Psalm 42.5

Forty and counting?

We live in a culture fascinated by numbers: News features are regularly pegged on some anniversary or other, and there are birthday cards to mark every decade. One in my possession depicts the 'A–Z of Forty'. Its 26 little illustrations range from Balancing Act and Downhill, through Midlife Crisis to Unshapely and Zinc Supplements! Forty, it seems, is the marker-point of change, or perhaps more accurately, the onset of decline.

Whereas the young are portrayed as attractive, able-bodied, sharp-minded, and able to enjoy life to the full, those of senior years are seen as past their sell-by date in a fast-moving consumer culture that continually trades in the old for the very latest model. Adverts and magazine covers broadcast the same message, giving the impression that nothing good ever happens to anyone over 25.

In such a context, ageing becomes associated with increasing obsolescence. No wonder reaching life's mid-point can trigger a crisis! If that is all we can look forward to, it makes sense to delay this stage as much as possible. Hence the growing movement to preserve the illusion of ageless youth, epitomized by the TV show, popular at the time of writing, that offers participants a full make-over package – including cosmetic surgery – just to pass themselves off as ten years younger.

Interestingly enough, 40 is also a significant number in the Bible, where it is often used, literally or figuratively, to represent a complete season or particular period of time: Noah was 40 days in the Ark; Jesus spent 40 days in the wilderness; there are 40 days between Jesus' Resurrection and his Ascension.

Forty years is also used to signify the span of a generation, though as we might expect, the biblical view of ageing is at odds with today's popular culture. From God's perspective ageing is connected more with fullness and maturity than uselessness and decrepitude. Age differs from youth just as the full-grown, fruit-bearing tree differs from the young sapling. Each season of life has its own beauty and purpose; what the older person lacks in physical vitality is offset by wisdom in those who have learned through their experience. Worth is more than skin-deep, and age is to be respected for its insights, not despised for its physical limitations.

The Bible does not appear to mark out midlife transition as a particular season of change in its own right, which might support the view of some that the midlife crisis is nothing more than a modern fabrication, an excuse for navel-gazing and irresponsible behaviour by those who should pull themselves together and simply 'get on with it'. So is the midlife crisis merely a mental self-indulgence for those who have just turned 40?

All in the mind?

At the beginning of the twentieth century, average life-expectancy was around 50 years old. With the high infant mortality rate and the longer period of child-bearing, the average woman was likely to be a widow by the time the last child married. Since then we have experienced 'two-thirds of the total gains in life expectancy since the human race emerged', according to midlife writer Gail Sheehy.[1] Moreover, with smaller families of children born closer together, there is still much life to be lived after these offspring have left home.

Some argue that with all this new time ahead, amid the comforts of a technological age, we have the leisure to indulge in the midlife crisis our forebears were too busy with basic living to be concerned about. Yet there is certainly no shortage of options for filling this time with activity, be it work or leisure. In a society that shuns ageing, we have the concept of the 'elastic life-cycle', where anyone can do anything at any age: fertility treatment can help post-menopausal women become first-time mothers; midlifers can take off with backpacks to travel on a student-style 'Gap Year'; widening educational opportunities bring adults back into the classroom; retirement is delayed, through choice or necessity; and Mick Jagger can still sing rock 'n' roll long after being pictured on the cover of *Saga Magazine*! As we reach 40 and the so-called 'Deadline Decade', we are told that through life-style opportunities and modern health and beauty care, '50 is the new 40', and the reality of ageing is put off for another day.

Yet the elastic life-cycle can bring confusion as well as opportunity. Behind all the bright lights and energy, we may find the activities of youth growing stale, as we experience a growing desire for something different. We are discovering that our tastes, appetites, desires, ambitions and outlook are shifting in ways we cannot quite yet define. The young ways are becoming old to us and do not satisfy us any more. Many of us have also found that life does not live up to all the spin.

We may argue that midlife issues are a relatively recent phenomenon, but if conversations with my contemporaries and counselling clients are anything to go by, they are very much a reality. If such issues are only spoken about in quiet voices, in counselling rooms or to trusted friends, it is because many feel that somehow life is not supposed to be like this. 'Perhaps it's just me who feels this way', people think apologetically. But many in middle adulthood are facing particular external issues alongside a deepening inner dis-ease about their own lives.

Two typical examples of midlife predicaments are illustrated by the situations of Keith and Karen, who represent the type of clients who can come through a counsellor's door at this time.

Keith is a manual worker whose increasing back pains mean he can no longer work – the result of habitually overdoing it when he has been employed. Home life is a strain as he feels his teenage children are not taking on the values of hard work and responsibility he has sought to instil in them. In addition, his ageing mother is increasingly frail and the family faces the decision of whether to put her into a Nursing Home. Keith used to feel confident and in control of life and head of his household; now he feels frustrated and weary.

Karen's husband left her for a younger woman, leaving Karen feeling like 'a cast-off old shoe'. Seeing the home in which they invested so much time and money broken up has been heartbreaking. She is also finding that the office job she has done for years has ceased to have meaning for her, and she wants to train as an aromatherapist (she finds alternative therapies and holistic spirituality increasingly attractive). But can she afford to do this and make ends meet now she is on her own? Karen feels both abandoned and trapped at the same time.

Keith and Karen typify the situations and issues that arise at midlife, and psychological research as well as experience points towards an understanding of midlife as a distinctive life-stage with its own unique characteristics.

Not so much an age as a stage

As the father of modern psychotherapy, Sigmund Freud's attention was very much centred on the impact of a person's early development on their personality. He even asserted that it was not worth anyone over 30 going into psychoanalysis as they would have amassed too much material in their life-experience to deal with adequately. It was his follower and ultimately independent psychoanalytic thinker, Carl Jung, who pioneered the notion of the midlife transition. As with much work of this nature, it was based on his own experience of personal upheaval between the ages of 38 and 43, though he identified it as a life-stage that could happen to anyone between the ages of 18 and 80.

Subsequent psychological researchers, psychotherapists and writers have developed and formulated themes and issues that seem to be characteristic of this shift, whether it takes place neatly within the 'Deadline Decade' of 40 to 50, or on either side of it. Perhaps you can identify with some of these midlife themes and concerns:

- boredom and/or restlessness
- changing tastes and new desires
- awareness of ageing
- feelings of vulnerability – life no longer seems so secure
- a sense of mortality
- seeing life in terms of time left not time ahead
- sandwiched between ageing parents and growing children
- feeling trapped by responsibility
- questioning the meaning of what you are doing and have achieved

- facing dying dreams and unfulfilled ambitions
- questioning the price you have paid to fulfil your ambitions
- becoming disillusioned with established wisdom
- weary with playing roles
- wanting to be the real you while you still have time
- finding spiritual life changing or emerging
- wondering what legacy you will leave for the next generation
- wanting to make a difference
- anxious to make your mark before it is too late
- a sudden awareness that you and those around you are not who they were
- a sense of urgency about living your unlived life – 'If not now, when?'

Crisis or transition?

While these issues could arise for anyone at any time of life, it is the particular combination of several of them together that makes the midlife transition distinctive. For some, midlife becomes a crisis; others make a smoother transition, in the same way that some youngsters go through adolescence relatively straightforwardly, while others experience enormous turmoil and ups and downs.

Midlifers who find themselves more at the crisis end of the spectrum are likely to be those for whom a traumatic event sparks the onset of the midlife experience. The unexpected loss of a loved one, job or one's health can suddenly threaten everything that has been taken for granted, pulling the rug from under the established adult's feet. If we have also had other losses or difficulties in our lives that we have not come to terms with or have avoided facing, midlife is more likely to fall upon us like a ton of bricks. The psychological researcher Daniel Levinson identifies 40 as signalling a significant time of transition, but comments that if this is not faced, the same issues may surface again at around 50 with even greater urgency and discomfort.

A particular difficulty for the midlifer, as opposed to the teenager, it that when problematic issues surface, the midlifer has to work things through in the context of established adult responsibilities at work and home. There is not the teenage luxury of being able to go off to the bedroom and slam the door when there is a meal to be put on the table, or a job to clock into! Facing midlife can seem like a lonely affair: complicated issues arise with seemingly little space to resolve them, yet resolve them we must if we are to become more mature and whole in our lives, instead of just older.

Creative change

At whatever age the midlife experience descends upon us, there comes a point when we realize we are moving into life's second half. Far from this being a stage to avoid, Jung claimed that midlife is the moment of greatest unfolding. He felt that this change demanded a radical re-appraisal of our whole way of being: 'We cannot live the afternoon of life according to life's morning; for what in the morning was true will at evening have become a lie.'[2]

Jung lamented that people seemed so ill-prepared to face and deal with midlife. He saw it as such a significant life-stage that there should be colleges set up for midlifers, where they could go to learn how to reorientate their way of living for their later years. For while the first half of life is characterized by growing physically and doing, the focus of the second half is the flowering of the personality and being.

Given that as Christians our life's journey is also a faith journey, we will want to turn to the Bible to look for what God's word has to say on the midlife season.

Three Old Testament midlifers

The Bible, of course, is not a manual but a narrative, so we cannot look up midlife crisis in an index in a search for designated guidelines. Yet within the unfolding story of God's relationship with his people – created, fallen, redeemed and renewed – we find individuals struggling with midlife issues.

King David's midlife struggle was marked by failure through giving in to a rash impulse. One fateful summer in his middle age, we are told that he did not lead his army out to war, as was the custom of kings, but stayed at home. Secure in his achievements and at the height of his personal power, David was resting on his laurels.

He seemed to have run out of challenges as he looked out from his palace with a sense of midlife ennui, idly watching the beautiful Bathsheba bathing. David had become used to having what he wanted and so he used his kingly power to possess Bathsheba. He then became morally compromised as he tried to reconcile his personal lust with his sovereign reputation, failing dismally in the process. In God's just and merciful dealings with David, David received forgiveness, but also had to grow up to take responsibility for his actions and live with the consequences. The baby born of his union with Bathsheba died, and strife never left his household again.[3]

For the prophet *Elijah*, there was the disillusionment of great triumph that seemed to have borne little fruit. Elijah had just done spiritual battle on Mount Carmel, defeating the false gods, yet despite this, he found himself a fugitive, on the run from the hostile Queen Jezebel. Here was the midlifer, sinking into the depression of wondering whether his life's work and efforts were ever destined to reap appropriate rewards.

As Elijah collapsed exhausted at the cave, God met him at the point of his immediate physical needs, before dealing with the deeper issues of his vocation, and emotional and spiritual life. Midlife is a time when we may need to acknowledge our whole selves, and pay more attention to how body, mind and spirit interrelate in our well-being. Elijah also expressed his sense of isolation and futility in God's service, albeit with some self-pity. In response, God challenged him to give account of himself, to dig deep and face tough personal questions: at midlife our capacity to resolve things through action can finally run out on us, forcing us to look inside for fuller answers.[4]

Job is a character who emerged with integrity through a midlife crisis that one could argue was engineered by God. His experience of sudden and traumatic loss brought him to the brink of an almost suicidal despair. Job's friends offered simplistic wisdom and tidy explanations for his predicament. But for Job, cosy theories about the causes of his misfortune did not square with the truth of his experience. Midlifers are often impatient with spin and the official version of events. Life has become too short to play with pretence, and they urgently pursue the reality behind the veneer.

Though Job's journey of exploration was agonizing, he was ultimately commended by God for honesty. Even then, he did not receive tidy answers to his suffering, just a call to trust in God's sovereignty. It is a characteristic of midlife that its resolution demands the willingness to live with some loose ends and raw edges; we realize that some questions have to remain unanswered. When Job received again what he had lost, he did so in the full knowledge that his security could rest in God alone. He had come through the midlife disillusionment of realizing that ultimately everything can be taken away, and gained a mature detachment from the things of this world.[5]

Midlife choice and challenge

These biblical characters illustrate varied responses to midlife dilemmas, from the self-destructiveness of David to the courageous faithfulness of Job.

As midlife issues manifest themselves on our ship of life, we have a choice: we can batten down our hatches and tune out the call to a deeper level of living; we can jump ship, making a wild and sudden change of job or partner as a way of restoring our youthful vigour; or we can go up on to the main deck, take hold of the wheel, and begin the adventure of steering a new course.

The midlife challenge is to learn to steer the ship we are on; to readjust our course, knowing we are already committed to the voyage. Yet within these limitations, we have the potential for making a creative transition, so that, far from being past our best, we can find that quality of life is more significant than quantity of years.

The Bible affirms life's seasons and stages, but the rhythm presented is one of growth, completion, death and Resurrection into the next stage, 'changed from glory into glory', as we journey closer to Christ.

Seasonal change at whatever stage is a process to be engaged with and worked through. The tree needs to burst its buds in order to come into flower; the flowers need to die for the fruit to develop; and as the ripe fruit is enjoyed, the tree needs a fallow time before the spring's new growth.

At midlife we come into high summer, with just a sniff of autumn in the air. Yet the eternal God is one who can break into life at any age or stage, renewing us and strengthening us so that we rise up on eagles' wings, just when we felt we were grounded for good. In the following chapters we will look at different marker-points of midlife, and consider our options for responding to them creatively.

Reflecting and responding

1 Think about the following questions:

- When do you think middle age happens? What criteria are you applying to answer the question?
- What is your attitude to being young and being old? Where do you place yourself on the spectrum?
- Have you noticed your own attitudes changing with age? In what way? How does it feel?
- Do you see behaviour and activity as 'age-appropriate'? Are there some things older people should not do (or younger people, for that matter)?

2 Consider the following differences in this word-list:

New   Fresh   Energetic   Innocent   Change   Adaptability
Handsome   Lively   Young   Questioning   Emptiness
Purpose   Weary   Wrinkled   Slow   Stamina   Urgency
Wisdom   Experience   Habit   Stability   Maturity

Put these into three columns of Youth, Middle Age, Old Age. Are there some that would fit in more than one column? What words and labels would you add? Do you feel one column is more desirable than another? What does that mean to you? Which for you are positive and which are negative?

3 Would you like to be 18 again? As you reflect on this, turn the thoughts and feelings that arise in you into prayer. Spend some time in quiet, listening for God's response. You might find it helpful to read Ecclesiastes 3.1–8 as part of this exercise.

2

Making peace with our past

Tired of trekking

'It was never meant to turn out like this', reflected the Traveller. He remembered how, once upon a time, he had left home at dawn with a spring in his step and energy in his young legs. Excited about the future, he had set his heart on his destination, mapped out his route, and committed himself enthusiastically to his course. He had breathed in the fresh morning air, imagining the sheer exultation of reaching his goal, and the fulfilment he would find along the way.

Yet now, after trudging through seemingly endless forest, the longed-for mountain-top seemed just a stale fantasy. The well-worn paths felt all too familiar – had he come this way before? Was he just walking round in circles? Doubt's damp fingers began to grip his spirit. He felt weary. Was it really such a good idea to go on following this trail? But where else could he go from here? He had travelled so far now his heart sank at the very thought of returning to start all over again. Besides, which was the way back?

No, he had committed himself to this enterprise. Well, some distant, younger version of himself had set this course, and trapped this weary, older self on a route he wasn't even sure he wished to continue. Sometimes he wondered if his younger self had been looking at the same map that now so oppressed him. How might it have been if he'd set out a different way that spring morning? Things seemed so changed in the twilight of summer.

The Traveller's legs were aching. His pack felt as if it were growing heavier with every step. He needed to sit down.

Julia McGuinness

The past is still, for us, a place that is not yet safely settled.

Michael Ondaatje

Never live in the past, but always learn from it.

Author unknown

I will repay you for the years that the swarming locust has eaten . . .
You shall eat in plenty and be satisfied, and praise the name of the
Lord your God, who has dealt wondrously with you. And my people
shall never again be put to shame.

Joel 2.25–27

How did I end up here?

An old joke tells how a group of tourists hail a local to ask directions
to their hotel. 'Well,' he replies, scratching his head, 'if that's where
you want to get to, I wouldn't start from here, that's for sure.'

Imagine the dismay on the tourists' faces. They are not in a suitable position for moving to their desired destination, but they are help-
less. Where else can they start from? This is where they actually are
now.

For the midlifer there can be a similar sense of disappointment.
There is no dice to shake, no 'chance card' to pick up to send us back
to square one in the game of life. We can only start from the position we have reached.

At life's mid-point we experience a growing awareness of our length-
ening past, and the increasing number of days already spoken for and
gone. As we look forward, the future now appears not as the time we
have ahead, but as time we have left; and when we look back, we can
find ourselves reviewing the wisdom of past decisions.

At midlife we start to view things from a new perspective, and see,
perhaps for the first time, how different we feel from when we first
set out on the path of adulthood. Changes within and around us that
we scarcely noticed as we walked through the years, now strike us with
force. Our personalities are developing, our tastes are transforming,
and what suited us well in our early adult life no longer seems to fit.
Values we once held dear have been tested and challenged by age and
experience, and perhaps been transformed in the process. Caught
unawares by the distance we have covered since our twenties, we can
be left feeling constrained by the current consequences of our early
choices.

Our restless midlife enquiry can feel not so much like a quest, but
more an inquest; our young self is in the dock, being called to

account by our older self. That decision on the threshold of adult-hood to pursue a particular career, ambition or relationship, to have this child, to turn down or take up that particular opportunity, was the start of the journey bringing us to where we are today. Yesterday's self chose a particular life-path without realizing that today's self might resent the limitations it would impose in years to come.

'Whatever gave that spotty youth the right to trap this middle-aged person into this job?' grieved a chiropodist, weary of looking at people's feet for a living. If he had known then what he knew now, he felt, he would never have sentenced his future self to a livelihood dulled by repetition.

Some, of course, may experience an opposite discomfort. Peter had never settled in one particular job, but enjoyed the variety and change of a succession of temporary contracts in different working environments. Free from the drive of ambition, he was sometimes the envy of colleagues committed for the long haul in their chosen fields. But by midlife, Peter was experiencing pangs of regret and self-doubt. How come he had adopted a lifestyle that meant letting slip opportunities to build and achieve something of substance? He felt as if he had made a series of short-term choices that left nothing to show for his years. What had once signified freedom now seemed merely an inability to commit.

We are also faced with the consequences of our relationship choices. Not only are we affected by life's changing ages and stages, so is our loved one. Once upon a time two young people with particular aspirations and dreams, needs and emotions, chose one another. And now we reflect on how different our relationship feels: loss of intensity may have been replaced by a deeper companionship, or we may sense that while we are still formally joined we feel personally less connected. Amid life's demands we may not have noticed our drifting apart. We wonder if that is desirable or even normal, and fear something has been lost. As Ruth told me, 'When I got married, we thought it was God's will. Now I wonder how much we've got in common. But I made a commitment, so I'm looking for ways to work within it rather than fight against it.'

For those who have experienced a series of relationships, there may be a sudden insight into patterns of involvement that have never developed beyond a certain stage of trust and intimacy. They may regret not breaking out of this repeating cycle, and fear something has been thrown away, while those who have remained without an adult partner may fear that something has never been found. Of course there are also those who at this stage may be left on their own wondering about the might-have-beens of a relationship prematurely lost through divorce or death.

And as we subject our past to this searching critique, time and distance add another dimension to our view of the landscape: the ways in which our life-situation itself limited the choices we were able to make. We may feel our options were so shaped and circumscribed that we never made an independent decision at all. Perhaps we never had a real chance to choose. Factors that can have a significant effect on the formative decisions of adulthood include:

- parental expectations
- quality of our home life and childhood experiences
- emotional needs
- health
- sudden change through bereavement or other loss
- influence and impact of other authority figures, e.g. teachers, youth leaders
- expertise of those advising us
- knowledge of our options
- financial circumstances
- opportunity

Seeing with the wisdom of hindsight that we were less in control than we realized at the time can leave us disillusioned with ourselves or angry at others. Yet we look back at midlife from a point of no return. Our task is to grieve the losses linked to our younger self, so we can regain the energy to move creatively through our current life-stage and beyond.

As we put our past under the midlife microscope, what we see may make this task seem daunting, but God is the God of the impossible, and offers us his compassion and companionship as we bring him our losses and limitations.

God meets the midlifer

God specializes in meeting people where they are, even when that is not where they have chosen to be or where he would have them remain: the Bible tells the story of God creating a race that chose early to go their own way, despite the devastating consequences. We do not start from the ideal place when it comes to our relationship with God, but by sending Jesus, God redeems our past, reconciles our present and restores our future in his purposes. Though he alone has the power to tear up the world and start again from scratch, God has chosen not to do this, but to find a way to come alongside us.

Jesus' ministry is full of encounters with lives that are not at an ideal starting point, yet to each he brings hope and healing as people respond to him: the woman who has suffered with the flow of blood over years is healed as she touches Jesus' garment; Bartimaeus, whose life has long been limited by blindness, is given sight; Nicodemus, who has made god-oriented choices from the knowledge he has, is challenged to receive his full spiritual sight, and be 'born again'.[1]

The redeeming of the past is perhaps best highlighted in the story of the disciples on the Emmaus road, after Jesus' death. Disappointed and disillusioned, they open their hearts to their unknown fellow-traveller. Step by step, the unrecognized Saviour explains how the Scriptures have foretold these latest events, enabling the disciples to see the past in a new light, through God's eyes. Places where they assumed he was absent, have actually been full of him all along.[2]

God is sovereign, even when we are caught up in events beyond our control, and whatever our strengths or weaknesses. Of course, it is not just on what has happened in our past that we reflect at midlife; it is also on what has never been.

Dying dreams

All of us have cherished dreams, from ambitions of being a great sporting hero, a high-flying professional, rich and famous, or maybe just founding a family or having a room of our own. But as the years go by we start to realize that some great dreams and youthful hopes may never come to pass. Or perhaps we have achieved what we set out to do, but the reality does not taste as sweet as it did in anticipation. Buzz Aldrin, who walked on the moon, famously came down to earth afterwards to experience 'the melancholy of all things done'. And if we have struggled and made sacrifices on the path to success, we may be left wondering whether it was worth the cost.

As we face the reality of where and who we now are, the future can look restricted: not only have past decisions and energies committed us to one unrepeatable course, they have also narrowed down our options. We may wish to leave the office for the medical profession, but at 50 it does not feel as though there is time left to re-train and embark on a completely new course. Once our choices seemed limitless, but now we sense we have much less room for manoeuvre.

So where do we go from here? We will turn more fully to the issue of the future in later chapters. For now, the focus is on the groundwork of making peace with our past. In this we still have some choices to make. We could set our smile, refuse to look back and determine to 'move on' – a popular phrase that can sometimes signify an avoidance of addressing painful and complex issues. We could try to hang on to our past, seeking to recapture our old enthusiasms for past pleasures, or try to repair our past by frantically rushing after the things we feel we have missed out on. But essentially our creative challenge at midlife is one of negotiation, of plotting a path between the extremes of denial and delusion. This is not defeat, but a mature integrating of our past into an acceptance of present realities, so we are set free to face our future. At some level or another, this will involve going through a grieving process as we mourn the younger self that has quietly passed away, perhaps without us really being aware of it. We may experience different emotions as we make this journey, and find ourselves going back and forth between them over a significant period of time (see Box 1).

All things working for good

It is sometimes easier to see God's hand over the whole of a life rather than from the immediate perspective of our own circumstances, yet the Bible shows us many ways in which God works at each stage of

---

**Box 1   Elisabeth Kübler-Ross's Grief-stages applied to the loss
of our younger self**[3]

Denial: I'm still exactly the same as when I was 22. This is just a bad
patch.

Anger: What a fool I was to do that course! It's my Dad's fault – he
was always pushing me.

Depression: It's too late to do anything now. You can't change the past.

Bargaining: If only I'd done it differently. I wonder what I could do to
turn back the clock?

Acceptance: I'm wistful about some of what I've left behind, but part of
my younger self still lives inside – and I'm glad for all I've learnt
along the way.

---

a life to fulfil his purposes, weaving in even the most unlikely material. Consider the following two examples:

Joseph was a product of his family background – his father Jacob shamelessly treated him as the favourite among his 12 sons. Not surprisingly, this familial dysfunction made its impact on Joseph and his brothers. While Joseph developed an exaggerated view of his own importance and destiny, seemingly underlined by certain dreams, his brothers were inflamed with jealousy. They sought to dispose of Joseph for good by faking his death and selling him to passing traders heading for Egypt. The future Joseph had imagined for himself could not have seemed more different. A season as Potiphar's slave was succeeded by unjust imprisonment, giving Joseph ample time for reflection on his early behaviour, and potential bitterness about his fate. Yet imprisonment was not Joseph's end. God used an unlikely chain of events, including further dreams, to lead to his becoming Pharaoh's right-hand man years later.

The tables were finally turned when Joseph's brothers arrived at court, hungrily seeking Egyptian charity at a time of famine. As they discovered the identity of the one on whose grace they now depended, the brothers felt doomed. At midlife, Joseph had come into the prime of his powers, yet had also matured in character enough to show mercy to his brothers (despite making them sweat a little!). 'What you meant for evil,' he told them, 'God meant for good.' Joseph may have felt powerless over his destiny, but even his brothers, who thought they were in control, discovered they were under God's gracious sovereignty.[4]

Paul was also a product of his background and upbringing: a Benjaminite, with a first-class Jewish education, he developed an understandable pride in his righteous qualities and religious qualifications. Paul's spiritual ambition led him ruthlessly to hunt down and persecute Christians. He even witnessed the murder of Stephen, the first Christian martyr. But Paul's zealous activism was rudely interrupted en route to Damascus when he was faced with Jesus himself, the very one he was persecuting.

Being on a mission to murder Christ's followers was not the perfect place for a future disciple to receive his commission. Yet that was precisely where the Lord chose to meet Paul, and while Paul later dismissed the value of his Jewish pedigree compared to the worth of knowing Christ, God did redeem this past. Paul used his Scriptural knowledge on missionary journeys across Asia Minor, as he engaged in Christian apologetics at the local synagogues.[5]

Both Joseph and Paul discovered that the sovereign grace of God works with, through and beyond all our choices and character faults, mistakes of immature judgement and even our wayward wills to further his glory and our good. Knowing that God is ultimately in control and acts with compassion, we can dare to bring our past under the spotlight and reflect on both our have-beens and our might-have-beens.

Piecing together our past

A major midlife question is, 'Who am I?' or perhaps more accurately, 'Who have I become?' Reflecting on our past can shed some light on this as we piece together elements that at first glance seem disparate. Clarifying some of the factors or people who have played a part in our decisions; finding connections between choices that seem un-

---

Box 2   Shaping my life

Draw a set of circles to list the jobs or occupations that have filled your time since you left education. Now see what lines you can draw between them to express a connection. For example, what is it you especially like or dislike about each one? What do they have in common? Do they demand similar skills or gifts? If you have only one circle, write inside or around it all the different elements this occupation has involved. Which have given you most satisfaction?

Draw two boxes. In one, list major decisions you have made that have changed your life. In the other, write the major outside events that have changed your life. Now draw two more boxes. Using the material in the first boxes, in one box put things that have worked out well; in the other, things you perceive, looking back, as negative changes. Did you feel this way at the time?

Draw a large triangle with the point at the top. Divide it into layers by putting lines across. In the bottom layer, write what you feel have been the most important influences in your life, going up to the least influential elements at the top. Note: you may have reacted to someone significant in your life by doing the exact opposite of what they wanted – that is also an influence!

---

related; gaining insight into some repeating or underlying themes that have characterized our course; all these can give us a grounding in who we are today.

At one Personality Type workshop I ran, a theologian suddenly saw a link between herself and her father. He was a mechanic, and she had always felt that their chosen paths in life were very different. But that day she realized she had inherited his passion for finding out how things worked, often by taking them apart in the process. It was just that her focus was how God has constructed the universe whereas his was motorbikes! This insight brought coherence to her personal story, and she was delighted to discover a connection to an aspect of her background that had previously puzzled her.

As you think about what has shaped your life within and without, you might like to pick up pen and paper and try the exercise in Box 2. Do not do it too earnestly – as you relax and play with the different shapes, you will be more open to making creative connections.

Making peace with our past

As we look back and face the truth about where we are and who we have become, our midlife task is to make peace with our past so that we can move forward freely. This involves gaining insight into our story; acknowledging the parts played by others in our lives, including God, and grieving our losses and missed opportunities. But it also involves recognizing our blessings, celebrating our achievements and being grateful for the personal resources our experiences have given us.

At first glance backwards, it is easy only to lament what might have been, as well as to see shortfalls, frailties and failures of our younger selves; but a more steady and reflective gaze will reveal the gains as well as the losses. Unlike the adolescent's black-and-white take on life, the midlifer has the advantage of maturity and is better able to work with a more complex picture.

We may begin to observe some benefits we have reaped from the choices we made – valuable treasures to salvage from the wreckage of our disappointments: relationships we have maintained, children we have had, compassion we have developed from the pains life has brought us; people we have met; experiences we have had, and what they have taught us; qualifications we have gained. And we can recognize and rejoice that our particular combination of those is unique.

A radio programme for the disabled once featured a discussion on whether it was better to place disabled children in mainstream schooling or to send them to a special school. The interviewee, who spoke positively about his experiences as a disabled child in mainstream education, was asked if he felt, looking back, whether it would have been better to have gone to a school more adapted to his needs. Did he feel he had lost out? 'That's a question you can't answer,' he replied. 'Nobody gets it all.'

Here was a man who wisely recognized the reality of life's limitations, and responded by holding on to the good he did have, rather than lamenting what he had missed out on. It can take time to reach that position: we may need to grieve over regrets of what might have been, before we can cherish some of the things we now have in their stead. Such a process will certainly mean accepting that some questions in our past can never be answered. We have to learn to live with the mystery: we are not to know what might have been.

Reviewing our past with more balanced vision will also mean looking at ourselves through new eyes and accepting the fuller truth that we are neither complete successes nor all-out failures, but something in between. We may not have achieved all our ambitions, but we do have some qualities and achievements to enjoy; we may have made some misjudgements, but these can teach us valuable lessons. The secret of successfully reviewing our past at midlife lies in both taking hold of some things, but also in letting go of others.

Letting go of baggage

As we reflect on our past we realize we are not just isolated individuals, but are linked to a legacy of early influences over us, from childhood onwards. Figures of trust and authority, from parents and teachers to friends and lovers, have affected us on our way. We may feel grateful for some aspects of their impact on us, but resentful of others.

We also need to face the fact that we will have made our mark on others: at midlife, we may need to acknowledge that alongside our creative side is a capacity for destruction. We need to come to terms with the damage we can do to people, and seek reconciliation and forgiveness.

Such a process is a key task at midlife – giving forgiveness and seeking reconciliation; receiving forgiveness and becoming reconciled with ourselves.

Baggage from the past can weigh us down on our life's journey, and midlife is a good time to release it if we want to walk on with a spring in our step. Forgiveness may not be an instant process: strong feelings of sorrow, regret, resentment and anger can surface when we begin to engage with such deep-rooted material, and we may need to seek the support of others as we work these things through.

Where we find we have unfinished business with another, we can offer forgiveness, apologies, or an opportunity for reconciliation. Sometimes it is not possible or appropriate to do this directly, yet we

---

Box 3   Seven essential 'Rs' in considering the past at midlife

- Review what has been
- Reflect on it before God
- Release old fears, resentments, dreams
- Recognize where God has been at work in the past and thank him
- Reconcile yourself with those people who have harmed you, and be reconciled to your capacity to harm others
- Relax as someone who is accepted as who and where you are now
- Respond to God's ultimate sovereignty over all that has been, as well as over what is to come

---

still need to find some way of resolving the matter within ourselves, perhaps seeking the help of prayer and counsel. We may not have chosen the way people have treated us, but at midlife we need to acknowledge our responsibilities in how we continue to respond – and make our choice about where we go with it, even if we did not want to start from here (see Box 3).

Reflecting and responding

1 Close your eyes and see yourself as the traveller presented at the start of the chapter. Imagine you are taking off the pack containing everything you are carrying on your life-journey.

Set it down and take the objects out one by one. What do you find, and what does each thing mean to you? What do you want to keep on carrying, and what would you rather leave behind? Are there some things 'unfinished', or that you want to pass on to someone else? Are there things to be accepted, or regrets to release?

Put back in the pack only what you want to take on with you. How can you leave the rest of your unwanted baggage behind? Are there things you need to do, or do you just need to let go and turn away?

2 Draw a 'map' of your route through life so far. What turnings and choices have brought you to this point? Chart the junctions where you made particular decisions, and the bends in the road where you had to follow the course of circumstances. Where might you have gone? What could you have done? Mark out what you regard as your losses on the map.

Now reflect on what you have gained on your particular route through life. What benefits and experiences do you value as you look? Add these gains to your map, and reflect on how they relate to your losses. What resources do you have now for the journey ahead?

3 Write a letter to someone you need to forgive, or apologize to, but cannot do so in person for one reason or another. Write what you need to express from your side to put the situation right and release your unfinished business.

You may find it helpful afterwards to shred or burn the letter, as a way of helping you to let go of the burden you have been carrying.

4 Write a letter to your younger self. What do you want to communicate? You might wish to express how you feel about the decisions your younger self made, offering forgiveness, understanding or thanks for the part this self has played in contributing to who and where you are today.

5 Imagine you are on your own 'Emmaus road', talking to Jesus about your past, with its disappointments, decisions and dreams. As you converse with him, allow some quiet space to listen for his insights into your past. Be willing to have your eyes opened to see things from a heavenly, rather than a human perspective.

If you prefer, you could write your words down, and leave a pause to write down what you sense Jesus is saying in reply.

3

Engaging with ageing

———◆◆◆———

IM39 TLC

My car needs more care now.
Once the glory of the multi-storey,
Now it sits, eclipsed by the latest model.
The bodywork has lost its early lustre:
Once pristine paintwork is nibbled with chips and scratches –
The price of going out into the world.
The right touch-up applicator paint helps, but sadly,
'Small difference in colour shade is unavoidable.'

My car needs more care now.
The engine has lost its eagerness on a cold morning:
Slower to start; quicker to grumble.
The MOT reveals more problems needing attention.
I guess it's just a Matter Of Time.
But increasing investment to stay on the road is inescapable, for
'Correct servicing and maintenance remains vital in
preserving reliability and safety.'

My car needs more care now.
Inner wear and outer tear on
The Drive of My Life.
But we're still companions for a few more miles on the clock.
There's life in my engine yet.
In parked privacy I scan my face in the inside mirror.
I need to adjust my make-up before stepping outside.
The right foundation evens my complexion, but sadly
'Small difference in colour shade is unavoidable.'

Julia McGuinness

To know how to grow old is the master work of wisdom, and one of the most difficult chapters in the great art of living.

Henri Frederic Amiel

Do not regret growing older. It is a privilege denied to many.

Author unknown

For everything there is a season, and a time for every matter under heaven.

Ecclesiastes 3.1

Face in the mirror

Janice said she knew midlife had truly begun the day she discovered an amazing new talent: she could vanish in public places. As she stood in the supermarket queue and realized that the young man nearby was not directing his admiring glance at her, but through her to the attractive twenty-something girl behind, Janice realized she had some-how transformed from young woman to invisible middle-aged lady.

Then there is the experience of John, who commented, 'When-ever I look in the shaving mirror these days, I see the face of my father looking back.' As someone who had not always related well to his father, this was a disconcerting sight for several reasons.

In a society where appearance counts for so much, we can feel dis-enchanted when our reflection radiates the unspoken message: 'No Longer Young', and when the compliment, 'She looks good', starts to be followed by, 'for her age'. Absorbed by the day-to-day, we can be unaware of gradual change, but there comes a defining moment when everything shifts, and we start to see ourselves physically in a new way. It is as if we catch up with these outer indicators of age all at once, through signs such as:

- skin becoming drier and gaining a few fine lines
- clothes getting tighter as 'middle-age spread' encroaches
- hair greying, going, or making unwanted appearances
- teeth yellowing
- once firm flesh slowly 'drifting South'

But it is not just our outward appearance that is evolving. As we catch up with the externals, changes in our physical well-being are more than likely catching up with us. We may well be increasingly experiencing:

- the menopause (or its hotly disputed male equivalent, the andropause)
- a change in libido and awareness of declining fertility
- less stamina and ability to spring back from partying and late nights
- niggling aches, pains and strains
- bodily chemical imbalances, e.g. diabetes, thyroid issues
- our first 'senior moments' as short-term memory stumbles
- having to hold books at arm's length or turn up the TV

At midlife we become more aware of our bodies than at any time since adolescence. Like the adolescent, the mid-olescent is dealing with a body changing through hormonal upheaval. For the adolescent this is connected with growth, but the mid-olescent faces decline. The result may be less acne, but just as much angst.

Assumptions we have made about our body's ability to look after itself without too much trouble can no longer be taken for granted, and health may become an issue. This could be in the form of an un-expected crisis or a long-term limitation we have to live with rather than be cured of – possibly the consequences of our chosen life-style. As one midlifer commented, 'I have to face the fact that I'll be taking tablets for the rest of my life.' This unexpected dependency disturbed him in itself.

Our body begins to demand more respect and take more time to recover from the demands we place upon it. Realizing our physical vulnerability can come as a shock as we struggle to accept that our body's ability to yo-yo back into form is gradually losing its 'yo'. As Carl observed about his ongoing back problems, 'I've had to learn that I'm not invincible.'

The menopause, a classic signifier of the point of no return, is a key biological change for women. However, it may be the emo-tional significance of the final loss of physical fertility that presents the greater challenge – or relief. The jury is out on the issue of male menopause, but both genders have to engage with the psycho-logical issues around chronological ageing and fears of waning sex-ual attractiveness.

Repairing the body beautiful

The psychologists Colarusso and Nemiroff have cited various mal-adaptive responses to the experience of having a changing, ageing body: alongside the attempt to get a new body by taking a younger partner, or acquire a 'substitute body' through buying a bigger house or new car, is the urge to repair the body through diet or cosmetic surgery.[1]

Today, the surgery pioneered for therapeutic reasons in response to the terrible injuries of the First World War, is a growing industry for aesthetic reasons, with such procedures no longer confined to the Hollywood elite. The number of women and men willing to submit to the surgeon's knife in pursuit of youthful looks may indicate the difficulty many have in coming to terms with ageing.

Others seek to prove their youthfulness by demonstrating their ability still to father or bear a child. While young mums may complain of feeling old and frumpy as they struggle in the early years of parenthood, the midlife writer Gail Sheehy comments that for some American women, having a baby can be a status symbol, a trophy for their youthful fertility. Yet not all can have prizes, and some of these super-fit, cosmetically enhanced would-be mums react with incredulous horror to the medical diagnosis that their eggs are too old for a viable conception. They have been living with 'fantasy of fertility for ever'.[2]

Midlife can also prompt a surge of interest in physical fitness – gym memberships for both sexes are soaring. But as midlifers don leotards, pound treadmills, heave weights and enter marathons to recapture levels of youthful energy, there is the danger of overexertion. The British Heart Foundation is not alone in warning against the dangers of a sudden increase in exercise in middle age: often the mind recalls past fitness levels more robustly than the muscles or joints! It is hard, but necessary, to respect one's own physical limits, as some overkeen midlife runners literally discover their Achilles heel – through contracting tendonitis.

Society may have a wry smile at the trout pout, the designer baby or the red-faced midlife athlete, but it gives people every reason to strive to reverse the effects of ageing.

In its obsession with youthful appearance, our narcissistic culture encourages us to look with lust, judge without love. This can leave many ill-equipped to face the reality of growing old, especially those whose whole sense of self is welded to body-image.

The psychotherapist Michael Jacobs suggests that 'there may be real difficulties for the self-absorbed person in midlife, when physical well-being begins to wane, illness becomes more common and the signs of ageing are more apparent.'[3]

Yet this is not to underestimate the real challenge faced by many at midlife, particularly those whose livelihoods have depended on their physical ability, beauty or agility, in addition to the basic health and fitness we may all have taken for granted up to now. But midlife stirs us to search more than skin-deep.

More than meets the eye

When God sent *Samuel* to choose Saul's successor as the next King of Israel, Jesse's sons were brought to him one by one. God did not select any of the brothers present, despite their fine looks, and warned Samuel not to be swayed by appearance or physical stature: Saul had once cut a dash, but his kingship had been a disaster because of his wayward character and disposition towards God. Eventually David, the remaining absent brother, was brought down from the hills where he was tending the sheep. Here at last was God's choice, whose handsome outward appearance matched an inner nobleness of heart.[4]

While at first glance we register a person's physical looks, apparent age and presentation, we see them differently as they become familiar. A face becomes linked to the whole person we have come to know, with appearance just one aspect of who they are. Intriguingly, the Gospel writers did not record Jesus' physical appearance. Perhaps in meeting him, they came to know such fullness in this perfectly whole human being that other details were peripheral. The loving depth of Jesus' gaze was a far richer encounter than could be encapsulated in eye-colour.

By midlife, experience will have taught us that a person's inner qualities count for more than mere muscle-tone or a date on a birth certificate, and seeing our own ageing reflection can prompt us to adjust our priorities. Midlife dismay that outer decline seems out of step with our unchanged inner feelings and desires can be turned into a determination to direct that energy inside to cultivate our character.

Much of the Bible's outlook on ageing runs counter to contemporary secular attitudes. Far from being simply about physical decline, ageing is seen as a continuing opportunity to grow towards maturity, accumulating the wisdom of experience to offer the younger generation. Age's potential treasures are affirmed as valuable and of unique worth, just as a maturing tree grows stronger with age, more securely established and able to offer shade to others.

Our life is a journey towards Christ-likeness and Christ himself, ultimately unimpeded by bodily limitation. Christians are those who are coming into fullness of life despite, or even through, physical decline. Besides which, declining physical vigour can be offset by greater spiritual and emotional stamina. And of course, we are loved throughout every stage of the lifespan given us.

With much of this thinking at odds with the world around us, our first task in coming to terms with ageing may mean being 'transformed by the renewing of your minds', as Paul urges in Romans 12.2, in order to see it from God's perspective. But reorienting ourselves to eternal spiritual priorities does not mean that physical issues are to be totally discounted.

Body matters

If Western secular culture's repair-response to ageing seems obsessively preoccupied with the physical, Western Christian culture has traditionally gone to the opposite extreme, by denying the body's value altogether.

The dualistic concept of separating of body and soul was inherited from the world of the Ancient Greeks. Plato and his followers made a radical division between the temporary physical body and the eternal soul dwelling within the outer shell. The latter was seen as vastly superior to the former. In the religious disciplines of the Middle Ages (as opposed to middle age!) this resulted in excessive fasting in order to purify the soul and subjugate the body and its lusts. The group of young female saints including Catherine of Siena have been called the 'holy anorexics' because of such practices.

The theological impact of dualism has continued down the centuries. Churches can reflect a punitive approach to things physical through an overcaution about sensual experience and enjoyment compared to spiritual enlightenment. Others have observed a new phenomenon among the rising postmodern Christian generation, in the ability to maintain two distinct modes of behaviour – one for the church fellowship and one for social circles outside. It is as if two different compartments of living have become disconnected from one another.

But the body is neither inferior nor irrelevant to our spiritual life and health. The Judaeo-Christian worldview is a robust embracing of the material world as God's good creation for us to steward and enjoy. We have been created to be whole people, integrated in body, mind and spirit. The Old Testament contains passages where God's people are commanded to celebrate in feasting just as they discipline themselves in fasting. Jesus, God in bodily form, both fasted and enjoyed shared meals, from wedding feast to homely hospitality. Indeed, his Resurrection body was not some ghostly apparition, but one that could be touched, could eat and enjoy a cooked breakfast with friends at a Galilean lakeside.[5]

As Christ's followers, we now embody his life: Paul reminds the Corinthians that the Christian's body is 'a temple of the Holy Spirit' and that we are to live with due respect for this inexorable link.[6] Since physical behaviour can have spiritual repercussions, he encourages his readers to 'glorify God' in the bodies that belong to their maker. As a Christian dietitian said to me, 'When I first read those words it really hit home, and I thought, "If my body's a temple, why am I putting so much junk into it?"'

The interconnectedness of body, mind and spirit is an insight we can become particularly sensitive to at midlife. We realize more fully that how we treat our bodies has an impact on our moods, energy levels, emotional and physical health, because our bodies are now quicker to tell us if we are overtaxing them. They also take longer to recover when we have burned the candle at both ends. Paradoxically, some of us only begin to value and respect our bodies as they start to let us down.

A more general growing awareness that we are whole people is reflected in the emergence of Mind, Body, Spirit fairs across the country. 'Spiritual spending' has been noted as a particular phenomenon among women approaching midlife, who are beginning to see bodily well-being as beyond beauty treatments. They are willing to part with cash in pursuit of alternative health treatments that soothe the mind, spirit and emotions as well as claiming to address their physical needs.

At midlife we can sense that within our ageing exterior lies an inner growing edge that we need to cultivate: true attractiveness begins with inner beauty, not a fashion statement. It is also the season when physical energy and the maturity of experience are perfectly counterbalanced. Making the most of midlife means learning to incorporate a greater respect for our bodies within a growing emphasis on developing our quality of character.

Bodily balance

Letting go of our youth does not mean 'letting ourselves go'. If the God who made us cares about us continuously, it is worth caring about our whole selves at each age and stage of life. We can present ourselves with style, pace ourselves with wisdom and prioritize with maturity as we face our ageing and make the best of who we now are.

Indeed, how we address our physical needs and outward presentation can say much about our inner state of being. Counselling clients regaining a sense of their own worth are often evidence of this: some gradually rediscover colour in their clothing, having initially come dressed in black or 'hidden' in baggy garments; others start paying attention to healthier eating patterns or establishing more appropriate rhythms of rest and activity.

It is said that a young man lives with his body, while an old man lives against it. However, we do not have to accept such stark alternatives. Successful negotiation of our life-stages lies in learning to adapt and adjust to changing scenarios. So the key words in a constructive response to the challenge of ageing at midlife are:

Acceptance *not* Denial
Balance *not* Excess
Integration *not* Alienation
Readjustment *not* Revolution

We need to make friends with our body rather than fight the inevitable, co-operate with reality rather than force the illusion that we can be the spring chickens we once were. It could be argued that Jesus' words in the Sermon on the Mount – 'Do not worry about your life, what you will eat or drink, or about your body, what you will wear' – might apply not only to a poor society's overanxiety about basic needs, but to a comfortable society's faddish preoccupations with retaining the appearance of youth.

There is a world of difference between running a marathon in a desperate bid to keep pace with the young, and running it for the personal physical challenge of making the most of what your body can still achieve. There is also a world of difference between dieting feverishly, tyrannized by the thought of 'illicit' food, and adjusting eating habits to maximize health and well-being.

Intense diets and punishing fitness regimes are not the stuff of midlife. We can use our knowledge and experience to develop a personally appropriate programme for our optimum physical well-being, instead of slavishly following the latest fix-all plan. Boxes 4 and 5 (overleaf) offer some principles you might apply.

Connections and confusions

As we seek to integrate body, mind and spirit with a new awareness of how each connects and contributes to our whole being, it is important that we also disentangle confusions. Attention to one aspect of our lives may dramatically change things in another. For example, a sluggish prayer time might simply be the result of trying to meditate too soon after a large meal! It is also worth considering whether:

Box 4 Moderating midlife eating: a gentle 're'-volution

1 **Re-establish** the purpose of food as for nourishment, not emotional comfort, punishment or reward. Find other ways of meeting non-nutritional needs.

2 **Remind** yourself of what, how and why you are actually eating by keeping a food diary for a fortnight to identify patterns you might want to adjust.

3 **Readjust** portion sizes and gradually scale down foods you find hard to eat in moderation.

4 **Relearn** the delights of taste and of enjoying your food: go for quality, not quantity.

5 **Re-educate** yourself into more healthy eating habits, such as increasing your intake of fruit, vegetables and water.

6 **Retune** to your body so that you can avoid being overhungry or overfull.

7 **Rebalance** your eating by savouring treats and special meals and then compensating by judicious cutting back over the rest of the week.

8 **Rediscover** the joys of cooking and preparing food rather than relying on readymade meals.

Box 5 Midlife movement ideas

1 Enjoy taking up a new form of exercise for enjoyment, not duty.

2 Pace yourself – phase-up activity gradually.

3 Incorporate movement into your daily life – relearn the joys of walking and stairs!

4 Think in terms of your personal best, not what a 20-year-old could achieve.

5 Enjoy a variety of activity, with different emphases – strength, flexibility, stamina.

6 Listen to your body – be aware of any particular vulnerabilities, aches and pains, and adjust accordingly.

7 Take your rest as seriously as you take your exercise.

8 Try meditation and relaxation exercises – learn the art of stillness as well as movement.

- we are using food to meet emotional needs;
- we are experiencing physical pains that are actually indicators of an imbalanced lifestyle, emotional or spiritual needs;
- we are facing spiritual blocks that reflect our emotional filters from past human relationships.

Aspects of our physical well-being can sometimes highlight other issues we have failed to address. We may need to relearn the skill of listening to our bodies, especially if we are used to having our mind on other things. For example, back pain might be a pointer to having taken on too many 'burdens', tension in the shoulders could indicate an anxious holding back of what we really need to express, and eczema might have something to say about what is getting under our skin! Not every physical symptom is a sign of something deeper, but it is worth staying open to what God might be saying through bodily means that we have not heard in other ways.

It may be that as we listen to our physical selves, we will pick up on issues calling out for our attention, before they have to shout more loudly through physical illness or stress burnout. Those of us who are conscientious and overcommitted can find it hard to limit our schedules if we are simply feeling fraught. It is only when we have a 'real' physical illness that we can allow ourselves to stop – but by that stage we may not have the choice.

Colin was working ever harder as he combined his regular job with a growing involvement in local radio. One night as he was 'doing 85 in the fast lane' in another dash up the motorway between commitments, he felt his arms tingling and found he could not see properly. Fearing this was a heart attack, Colin pulled over to the roadside. He crawled out and sat on the car bumper for 15 minutes before managing to stagger to a nearby phone box to call the emergency services. He was off work for over a month, but though the medical profession ruled out a heart attack, they could not find out exactly what was wrong, beyond a general diagnosis of a stress-related crisis. But Colin knew his body was finally giving him a wake-up call. He had to hear the message about his physical limits, and decide which of the two 'jobs' he was going to pursue.

Body and spirit

If God can communicate to us through our bodies, then we can also 'speak' back to him in ways beyond words. We can explore the use of posture and movement in prayer; we can use our physical senses to tune in to the presence of God through Creation. Physical actions – lighting candles or holding stones – can become meaningful ways of bringing body and solidity to our prayers. We can explore ways to give form to Paul's injunction to 'present our bodies as living sacrifices'[7] in new expressions of worship. We may also take stillness more seriously in our prayers.

> *Liz Babbs*, a self-confessed activist Christian writer, discovered meditative prayer through the enforced pain and passivity of ME.[8] She confesses she had had 'no idea that Christian meditation and contemplation were such powerful forms of prayer. The deep relaxation and quality of rest I experienced were incredible.'
>
> Back in active health, her vulnerability to overworking ultimately resulted in stress burnout. She now knows the need to listen to her body and incorporate stillness into her schedule, and make some wise choices about how she paces herself. She confesses this is not always easy:
>
> 'You have to live through a certain amount of discomfort if you want to change ingrained habits. I'm having to retrain my thoughts and whole approach. Each day I take time to pray the Lord's Prayer slowly and reflectively, combining it with calm breathing in and out. I'm rediscovering how this way of praying works when I discipline myself to do it.'

Coming to terms with ageing at midlife brings us into a new relationship with the body we can no longer take for granted. We will need to give it more attention, but will also set less store by its appearance as the ultimate measure of our attractiveness. We can gain a deeper appreciation of how our body, mind and spirit interrelate, and integrate our physical life into our spiritual life in new ways. And while we may not have the capacity for the quantity of activity of our younger adulthood, we can make this work for us by some wise reprioritizing, so we do what matters and make it count.

Ageing brings humility as we acknowledge our limitations and dependence on our maker; but through it we may find a deeper relationship with the Lord of our whole being.

Reflecting and responding

1 Give some quality time to your body by creating your own 'health spa' day, such as through healthy eating, gentle exercise, a fragrant bath etc. How does it feel to lavish attention on your body?

2 Try a whole prayer time using bodily movements and postures rather than words. You might like to take the Lord's Prayer or another well-known prayer or hymn and express each line with a physical action.

3 Adopt and hold an appropriate posture while you speak different parts of your prayers, such as adoration, thanksgiving, confession, intercession for others, personal petition.

4 Practise a relaxation or meditation exercise where the object is to become completely still. What happens as you take time to come into quietness?[9]

4

Looking outside in

Stop!

I'm worked up, hyped up
keyed up, bound up
tied up, screwed up
fed up, wound up!

I keep on striving . . .
wanting to win
want your applause
want to be thin!

One day I'll succeed . . .
if I only try harder.
One day I'll be perfect . . .
if I only pray harder.
One day I'll deserve love . . .
if I only work harder.

I want to slow down,
but I'm too scared to stop.
I'm afraid you won't like me
when I let my mask drop.
I need to wear hats
so I know who I'm being.
I want to keep busy –
it's safe to be *doing*.

When I take off my shoes
and stand naked and bare,
I'm afraid I'm invisible –
that there's no ME left there.

God,
I want to lie down,
I *so* want to rest.
I want to sink down
like a child on your breast.

Teach me to stay – not run off and hide.
Teach me to nurture the person inside.
Help me to find the centre that's still.
Let me make space for my maker to fill.

Sue Mayfield[1]

What can we gain by sailing to the moon if we are not able to cross the abyss that separates us from ourselves? This is the most important of all voyages of discovery, and without it, all the rest are not only useless, but disastrous.

Thomas Merton

It is a great grace of God to practise self-examination; but too much is as bad as too little.

St Teresa of Avila

When I was a child, I spoke like a child, I reasoned like a child; when I became an adult, I put an end to childish ways. For now we see in a mirror, dimly, but then we will see face to face. Now I know only in part; then I will know fully, even as I have been fully known. And now faith, hope and love abide, these three; and the greatest of these is love.

1 Corinthians 13.11–13

The sandwich generation

'You're an old fogey now!' the child shouted out to her aunt, who was strutting her stuff on the dance floor at her fiftieth birthday party. This child's-eye view of her aunt's half-century celebration was taken in good part, yet despite their growing distance from the younger generation, midlifers can feel unready to enter the senior circle. And for every teasing youngster, there is an older person saying ruefully how they wish they still had the youthful vigour of a 50-year-old.

They say two's company and three's a crowd, and some think this especially applies to a family with three children. Often the middle one feels the squeeze most, as he or she faces the challenge of establishing a distinctive identity and role. Neither the prized eldest nor the cherished youngest, the middle child can feel out of sight, overshadowed by both siblings. This pattern is echoed in the wider scenario of the three generations: young, middle-aged and old. Living between the emerging generation and the retiring one, the midlifer can feel submerged in the centre.

Where we are in the scheme of things can become an issue. Unable to identify wholly with either young or old, we are left at a loss to know what our identity 'should' be. We know who we are not, but cannot quite grasp who we are. Yet there is no such uncertainty about what we do.

Like a sandwich-filling, midlifers may be less visible, but provide an essential element of nourishment in the middle. They can find themselves stretched both ways by the needs and demands of those at either end of the age spectrum.

Those with children are likely to be experiencing their offspring at the draining stage of adolescence, a major transition in its own right. Dealing with challenging behaviour from those on the sometimes rocky road from child to adult is unsettling for parents coming into their own personal phase of questioning.

Some midlifers in the early stages of grandparenthood may be supporting two generations. Others, who represent the trend for later parenthood, may find, as Mark did, that the birth of a baby in itself can precipitate a midlife crisis: 'You feel so aware of your mortality when you see this little person who's going to outlast you by 40 years. You also start wondering what you and the rest of mankind are doing to the world, and what sort of an inheritance will be left for your children.'

The arena of work, traditionally regarded as a male domain (as the home network is seen as more central to a women's sphere of operation), is also a place where the 'middle man' takes the flak. For the first time, a rising generation of ambitious young workers is ready to move into the midlifer's shoes, potentially leaving him or her with nowhere to go. Working life continues, with the remaining rungs on the career ladder vanishing, but retirement not yet on the horizon. The Damoclean sword of redundancy swings in the shadows as a particular threat at this stage, especially where dependants may be affected. Responsibility for others can weigh heavily on midlifers' shoulders as they try to navigate their course through the currents of changing relationships at work and home. This can also inhibit them in making desired life-changes that involve risking their livelihood.

Yet the older generation also require support: parents of mid-lifers may be in their own stage of transition, which makes a profound impact. The once vigorous authority figures, who offered protection and a point of reference for their offspring, start becoming older and frailer. For midlifers, this means more relationship readjustment as they take on a new level of responsibility for their parents, the pro-tector becoming the protected. Relinquishing a parental role on the one hand while picking it up on the other may lead to some dis-orientation in the middle.

The issue of parents' mortality, either in prospect or in actuality, also touches deep feelings. Another barrier between ourselves and the ultimate realities of life and death is being removed. As one couple observed after both sets of parents died over a short period of time, 'We're now the front line.' While the death of one's parents is not necessarily a midlife experience, their changing and ageing inevitably prompts personal reflection whenever it happens. The death of a par-ent may trigger the midlife experience, as much as the birth of a child: such events pitch us into the meaning of life beyond the day-to-day round.

Roles

Shifts in our intergenerational relationships can bring to light how much we are caught up in different roles at home and work.

As we grow up we discover what we need to do to survive, make an impact, gain approval and succeed. We develop roles in our per-sonal, social and working life to ensure we are accepted, secure and recognized, as well as protected in our more vulnerable areas. In the first half of life, these roles help us establish our identity and status in the outer world.

Roles serve a useful purpose: we know what to do, what to wear and how to behave; we can measure our success by our achievements; fulfil the expectations of others and establish a clear way of defining our identity. It is interesting to note how, when we introduce ourselves to one another, we often talk about what we do.

By midlife, most of us have several roles relating to different aspects of our lives, and managing them can be a growing source of frustration. It is more common for women than men to come into counselling at this stage, complaining of 'role overload' (as parent, worker, home-maker and perhaps committed church member), though both sexes can struggle with the multiplicity of roles or the punishing demands of one in particular.

We may have acquired roles that we do not actually like, but have given us recognition – from Golden Boy to Black Sheep, Coper to Victim, Performer to Conformer. However, whether we have welcomed our roles or had them foisted upon us, we discover that what has helped us outwardly is beginning to obstruct the person we are inwardly. We can find ourselves becoming resentful, rebellious or just plain weary.

Whatever activities, behaviour and expectations we have taken on board, no role can encompass all we are. By midlife this realization can lead to a restless longing to live more meaningfully; outer demands may feel suffocating as our inner life claims our attention. We want to break out, perhaps as our outer roles are breaking down; to live authentically and be true to our own inner values and priorities instead of chasing others' needs and agendas.

For Carl Jung, this shift from outer to inner is the hallmark of midlife transition. The second half of life is the time for the flowering of the personality, a growing into wholeness. He describes our outer functioning self as a persona – the Greek word for an actor's mask. This mask is 'designed on the one hand to make a definite impression on others, and, on the other, to conceal the true nature of the individual'.[2]

Do we dare take off our masks to expose our real face? It can take courage to look behind our different roles, instead of soldiering on with the status quo of meeting expectations and keeping others happy. Fulfilling a role at least gives us some immediate reward.

To step out of it means letting go and journeying into unknown territory.

Jung tells the story of a stressed individual who sought his help. He advised the man to take some daily time alone. Weeks later the man returned, excited at his 'progress'. He described how he spent the prescribed time in his study, listening to music and reading books. Jung responded: 'But I did not tell you to spend time with Mozart and Shakespeare, just with yourself.' 'I can't imagine anything worse,' replied the man. 'But', replied Jung, 'this is the self you inflict on everyone else all day long.'

However we feel about our roles and our doing, they do protect our being – from others' intrusion and from our own deeper self-knowledge. Roles may even offer the appearance of liberation, like the unruly team mascot clowning around on the pitch, with no inhibitions or sense of responsibility. But true freedom is the freedom to be totally who we are without dressing up and hiding from ourselves or the consequences of our actions.

Into the light

The Christian journey is a walk into the light, until all we are becomes known to others and ourselves as it has always been known to our maker. Each step along the way is part of the journey into wholeness, as we allow what comes into the light of God's grace to be accepted, redeemed and transformed according to how he originally purposed us to be. We are called to co-operate in this change 'from glory into glory'.

The call to bring to light the essential person underneath our roles is a key midlife task on this walk of faith, and how we respond has long-term consequences. If we play safe and continue as we were, our masks may become even more glued to our faces. We all know those who have come to the end of what they 'do' – through retirement or the end of parenting – and are unable to get in touch with any other part of themselves than the one that has done the job. Yet ultimately all roles leave us, so it is vital to nurture the person we are underneath, however uncomfortable the process. Midlife offers the opportunity to face our real selves in the mirror, while we have time to respond creatively to what we see. We can reflect on the various roles we have amassed. What would it mean to let them go? Have we developed what is inside, or fed our outer demands?

Through life's changes and losses, God allows us to face who we are when the externals fall away, as he holds us in his enduring, all-knowing love. Though we may at first feel things are falling apart, we can eventually ground ourselves more securely in our createdness and belovedness in Christ, rather than in an attachment to what we do, have or achieve. You might want to ask yourself who you are without:

- a partner
- a child
- a job
- a position in the church
- a bank account
- a treasured possession
- a home
- a healthy body
- a full diary
- a computer, car or telephone
- a passport
- a room of your own?

The loss of some of the above can feel very threatening. The feelings expressed by victims of the growing crime of identity theft, for example, evince a stronger sense of personal violation than suffering the stealing of property. Yet who we are is ultimately not defined by PIN numbers or passports, or even a state identity card.

Midlife is characteristically the season when we find ourselves reflecting on these things: as one midlifer, dazzled by the details in the offer of his new company car, said, 'There's a little voice inside me that keeps on saying, "It's only a car." ' Little voices can raise big feelings, but if we have the courage not to squash them into silence, they can usher us into a deeper, richer attachment to Christ that will remain when we finally have to detach from everything else at life's ending (see Box 6, overleaf).

Box 6   Nebuchadnezzar

Nebuchadnezzar experienced a radical change through the temporary loss of his position, status and even humanity. Amid the comfortable splendour of his Babylonian palace, he was disturbed by a recurring dream of a magnificent tree cut down to its stump and roots. When summoned, the prophet Daniel discerned that the tree represented the King himself, and its fate foretold God's plans for Nebuchadnezzar. Sure enough, as Nebuchadnezzar savoured the sight of his capital city Babylon, built through his power and reflecting his glory, God chose to humble his pride and remind him that the source of all blessing was God himself.

The King was driven away from human society, to live among animals and become as one of them through being deprived of his rationality. Yet God held him through the process, and in due season restored Nebuchadnezzar's former wealth and status. The monarch testified that through this experience, his outlook was utterly transformed into one of humble dependence on the true King of Kings.[3]

Looking inside

Taking on a role is not wrong in itself: Jesus took on the role of the world's Redeemer, the Servant-King. In doing this he was not acting a part but fulfilling a purpose that flowed out as an expression of his essential character and nature.

Luke tells us that at Jesus' baptism, God's voice from heaven confirmed his identity – 'You are my Son, the Beloved; with you I am well pleased' – rather than issuing a job description. The temptation in the wilderness immediately following both tested and confirmed this identity. Stripped of all external stimulus and provision for 40 days, Jesus emerged from the desert secure in the knowledge of who he was, and ready to move out into his mission. So often human beings try to do things the other way round!

Throughout his demanding earthly ministry, Jesus took time out alone to pray, reaffirm and deepen his connection with his Father, and simply 'be' God's Son. At midlife, we can feel a stronger impulse to step out of the hurly-burly to become more deeply grounded in who we are in God. Space and solitude become more essential to

OPEN What is known to us and to others	BLIND What is unknown to us but known to others
HIDDEN What is known to us but unknown to others	UNKNOWN What is unknown to us and to others

Figure 1 Johari's window

well-being, and need to be incorporated into the rhythm of our daily living.

Paul concludes his inspirational words about love in his first letter to the Corinthians by observing that though his current vision is like seeing 'in a mirror, dimly', he will ultimately 'know fully, even as I have been fully known'.

As fellow pilgrims, we share this destiny as we travel deeper into the light and love of Christ. The midlife desire for more meaningful relationships beyond our roles can be a significant marker on our way.

Without a sense of being held in his enduring love, fully knowing and being fully known to God could feel like a daunting prospect. Moreover, growing in self-knowledge is no simple task: it is helped and hindered by our relationships and roles in life, as well as affected by our own response to past personal experiences. Johari's window highlights the limitations of our self-knowledge – we all comprise its four elements (see Figure 1).[4]

While God sees through the whole window, we only see – and prefer to be seen – in part. Christian maturity involves letting in more light, as we face the call to live more authentically that presses upon us with greater urgency at midlife.

What might it mean to expose more clear glass in the window's 'Hidden' section? We could learn to 'let our yes be yes and our no be no', instead of adjusting our response to what we think others want to hear; seek ways of appropriately offering our true opinion, without conforming to or reacting against the majority view; address whatever needs to be put right in our own life, so we have less that we feel compelled to hide; take new risks of trust with those around us.

Gaining vision through the window's 'Blind' section is more complex, as it encompasses aspects of ourselves of which we are unconscious. Since we do not know what we are looking for, we depend on these things being revealed.

This can happen by being ready to listen to feedback from others, and perhaps being willing to ask for it. We might also start to tune in to the things others volunteer about us. For example, are there things people are 'always saying' to us? Taking time for prayerful reflection might help discern some patterns that reveal a few underlying truths. Talking through these issues with a trusted other as we seek to become more in touch with the truth about ourselves can be uplifting as well as sobering: we may well discover unrealized gifts and talents alongside unwelcome weaknesses!

The window's Unknown section presents the greatest challenge, for what is obscured here is unconscious material, concealed from both ourselves and everyone else. Yet it significantly affects our everyday lives and relationships, despite our lack of awareness.

The Unknown may include material inherited from our parents and early experiences, before conscious memory; unrealized connections between our present and past; or areas we have placed out of conscious reach because they are too painful or awkward to keep in mind.

At midlife, we may want to retrieve some of this hidden material as we turn from the frontiers of the outer world and realize that there is a whole new territory to explore within our own being. We become newly amazed at human complexity, and the fact that we are so 'fearfully and wonderfully made', as the Psalmist observes in Psalm 139.

There is the danger that exploring our inner world can become such a fascinating enterprise that we descend into self-centredness, but as the Psalmist continues, he invites God to: 'Search me . . . and know my heart.' This is no indulgent introspection. God is asked to open up deeper self-knowledge to the Psalmist for a purpose: 'See if there is any wicked way in me, and lead me to the life everlasting.'

Gaining such self-knowledge can enable us to grow in wisdom on our Christian journey into love and truth, if we consciously offer what is revealed back to the Lord for redemption and healing.

Human feedback cannot help us with the Unknown, but divine feedback, in the form of revelation and insight, can. As the Psalmist declares to God: 'You were there when my inward parts were formed in the womb . . . Such knowledge is too wonderful for me; it is so high, I cannot attain it.'

But how does God reveal what he wants us to know about ourselves? Like the Psalmist, we can pray for insight. But at midlife, it may be more a case of listening to what is already trying to make itself heard from inside.

Stirrings from the deep

If we have locked children away in a basement room, sooner or later (probably sooner!) they will make a noise to persuade us to set them free. The longer we ignore them, the louder they shout. By midlife, aspects of ourselves that we have pushed down below begin to turn up their volume.

Perhaps this is a natural God-created movement in our psyche towards wholeness and integration. For by midlife, we have by and large established a sufficiently secure outer life to gain the strength to look within. As we become more ready to search for the truth, the truth comes looking for us.

The Unknown may make its presence felt through a growing dissatisfaction with living out roles that are disconnected from who we essentially are. As the strain of doing this increases, we become weakened by weariness and eventually cannot contain the inner life any longer. The warning here is that if we do not heed the rumblings within, inner issues may erupt with enormous force: just like those children confined for too long in the basement, they may finally break out to run riot, until we manage to settle them down and accommodate them into our home. We need to address any feeling of fracturing between our roles and our real selves, rather than risk rupture.

The Unknown may include aspects of ourselves that we are uncomfortable with and struggle to own. Reflecting on the questions in Box 7 (overleaf) could help identify submerged material from some surface hints and glimpses.

51

Box 7   Eight spotlights on the shadow

1   What do I forget, or habitually arrive late for?
2   Where do I get nervous, anxious, sensitive or touchy?
3   What can I not tolerate being wrong about?
4   When do I find myself feeling inferior or lacking in confidence?
5   What do I rarely talk about with other people?
6   What kind of people do I have the greatest dislike for and difficulty with?
7   What positives or negatives do people point out to me that I find hard to accept?
8   Where am I most dissatisfied with myself?

Another way the Unknown can break through is via recurring dreams. When we are unconscious and our guard is down, deeper concerns begin to find expression. Images and feelings can be particularly strong and disturbing, but God is God '24/7', and can contain every aspect of our lives.

Moreover, the Bible takes dreams seriously. God uses them as a way of communicating – consider the role they play in the Nativity story. As we bring our dreams to God in reflective prayer, we can seek his insight about what he wants to bring to our attention. Most dream material concerns the dreamer's own issues. Where other known people feature in the night-time drama, it is most helpful to start by considering prayerfully what they represent for us or in us. We can also reflect on any links we can make between the feelings experienced in our dreams and our waking emotions. Such connections may well reveal areas that need addressing directly. Pursued prayerfully, and perhaps with a wise soul-friend, we can find God helping us to see more through our Unknown window pane.

Shadowlands

God is Lord of our shadow, and wants to make us whole by bringing things to light. A final element of our Unknown may simply be ways of living we have not developed because we have preferred the alternative.

The Myers-Briggs Type Indicator highlights the distinction in our personalities between our preferred and least-preferred approaches to life, from our attitudes to our inner and outer worlds, to our perceptions and decision-making.[5] For the first part of life, we tend to rely on our preferred ways of doing things. We play to our strengths, and enjoy using those aspects of ourselves that come naturally to us. This may be at the expense of our least-preferred sides, which may become left in the shadows. But at midlife, aspects of our neglected, unlived life make themselves felt, to enable us to become fully developed, whole and balanced personalities.

Many midlifers wonder if they are changing personality as they sense new aspects of themselves emerging and seeking integration. In fact, they are not fundamentally changing, just developing and rebalancing. This process is a gradual integration of the different aspects of our personalities into a balance of both/and, not either/or. Yet on the way, midlifers might experience it as the loss of effectiveness of something they have always found helpful – from a style of worship to a particular career, or the emergence of a new appetite for things that have never previously appealed – from gardening to amateur dramatics! Box 8 (overleaf) offers some more general possibilities for changing tastes and preferences.

God at work

At midlife we may feel urgently prompted to step back and reappraise our roles. Far from pitching us into a spiral of introspection, space and time to get to know ourselves better in the light God sheds on us can create a surer foundation for more authentic relationships with ourselves, with others and with God. Being our true selves, the self that God made us, is the one job we cannot delegate to anyone else, so we need to give it some appropriate attention.

God works beyond what we can ask or imagine, even in our unconscious, but we are called to co-operate with him: 'Work out your own salvation with fear and trembling,' writes Paul, 'for it is God who is at work in you.'[6] For this to happen, we need to be aware of what we need to address, and ready for God to bring it to light. But as we answer the call to discover more deeply who we really are, how

---

Box 8 Changing tastes and preferences

- If you have preferred the inner life of reflection, you may have a new desire to go out into the world and party!
- If you have been a get-up-and-go type, you may find a growing taste for solitude or just a few friends, to restore your soul in quietness.
- If you have been a dreamer, always thinking of the future, you may find new pleasures in the experiences of the senses, and an awareness of the present moment.
- If you have been one for always doing things by the book, you may want to launch out and do something creative to break the mould.
- If you have been one to make the tough decisions, you may find yourself beginning to value hearing other people's feelings before ploughing on ahead.
- If you have always kept the peace, you may discover the value of saying no to people, even when you disappoint them.
- If you have always been an organized person, you may begin to explore being spontaneous.
- If you have always gone with the flow, you may find times where you want to commit and see something through to the finish.

---

do we deal with what emerges? How do we move from roles to reality? In the next chapter we will explore ways of moving on in the midlife journey.

Reflecting and responding

1 Draw a central circle on a piece of paper, and lines out from it to different circles drawn to represent your various roles. What do you do in each of these roles? Where do you feel frustrated by them?

  What aspects of you are concealed from others beneath these roles? Write these in the centre circle. What aspects of you flow into these roles and are expressed through them? Write these in all the relevant circles. Do these aspects have things in common? What patterns emerge? What adjustments might you want to make in response?

2 Reflect on how the different sections of Johari's window apply to you personally. Be as honest as you can about both strengths and weaknesses. If you dare, ask for feedback from two trusted friends from different areas of your life. How does their view compare with yours? Do they see qualities that you have missed?

  Pray together and listen to God to see if he brings anything further to mind. Surround this activity with a focus on God's unconditional love to protect any feelings of vulnerability.

3 Consider the people and issues that get under your skin. What or who are you totally unreasonable about? Whose behaviour in your life really gets your goat? Reflect whether there is something about them that is actually true of you. Are they letting themselves do things that you do not allow yourself to do? Can you take responsibility for your reaction and choose a different way rather than criticizing or losing your cool?

4 Explore some less familiar ways of praying: if you usually prefer solitude, go for a prayer walk in your local market. If you generally rely on prayer lists, spend some time simply being still before God, either in silence or using some gentle music. If you enjoy theological analysis, take a piece of plasticine and model it with your fingers to express your prayers. If your prayers tend to focus on people, find a piece of Scripture and tease out a tough theological issue. Can you sense God meeting you through these different means of relating to him?

5 Keep a dream diary for a while. Are there any recurring patterns? God can speak to us while we are asleep. Dreams may highlight issues we need to address but have ignored or pushed aside during the daytime. Pray about your dreams, alone or with a partner, and ask for God's insight.[7]

5

Living inside out

◦•◦

Living off centre

Like a wooden spinning top
With its main mass lopsidedly near the edge,
I have wobbled erratically
Weaving an uncertain
Inconsistent
And unstable
Course
Through life so far.

I have lived life inauthentically
Off centre
Away from the core of my being
Not constantly tapping into the well
Of my being.
I have not invoked my vocational
Mystery, endowed by the Eternal One.
At an early age an obscuring
Of the centre, was made manifest.

Now in middle age, early forties
I want to spin, dance truly
From my centre,
So I am still, yet turning
To the Source of life within and beyond.
                              Glyn Brangwyn[1]

One of the marks of a mature person is the ability to dissent without
creating dissension.

                                        Don Robinson

If we stand in the openings of the present moment, with all the length and breadth of our faculties unselfishly adjusted to what it reveals, we are in the best condition to receive what God is always ready to communicate.

T. C. Upham

For he is our peace; in his flesh he has made both groups into one and has broken down the dividing wall, that is, the hostility, between us.

Ephesians 2.14

Divided Kingdom

King Rehoboam, son and successor to King Solomon, was approached by the Israelites as he began his reign. 'Your father made our yoke heavy', they complained. 'Lighten the hard service of your father . . . and we will serve you.'

The King sought the advice of two groups: the older men, and the younger generation.

The older men counselled the fledgling King Rehoboam to serve the people and 'speak good words to them', to secure their loyalty and support. The younger men were for a more forceful approach. They advised the King to declare strongly his intention to add to the yoke already borne by the people, and indeed, where Solomon had used whips, to intensify the discipline 'with scorpions'.

The King took the young men's advice. Rather than win the people over, he proved he had not listened to them at all. The result was rebellion, and King Rehoboam had to withdraw to Jerusalem to rule over Judah, while the Israelites anointed his rival Jeroboam as their King. The once united Kingdom became divided.[2]

As we look at our own inner Kingdom at midlife, we evaluate our inheritance from the past amid the realities of present circumstances. But we will need to move beyond the impulsive counsel of youth and apply the wisdom of experience if we want to avoid wars within and without.

Black or white

The psychoanalyst Melanie Klein concentrated on the stages of very early childhood, and her theories interpret an infant's primitive reactions to its mother. When she is on hand to fulfil the infant's every need, total satisfaction is experienced from this 'good' mother; when she is not immediately available, the infant experiences total abandonment and rejection, resulting in rage at the 'bad' mother. These all-compassing reactions, known as the paranoid-schizoid position, form what we might call a black/white, or totalizing response. The universe is clearly categorized into goodies and baddies. The childhood world of the fairy tale offers the alternative of 'happy-ever-after' endings for the good, but punishment for the wicked. The adult world of the tabloid newspaper story is not dissimilar.

Yet the goal of maturity, Klein argues, is to move beyond this into what she describes as the 'depressive position'. This is not to be confused with depression, though it involves some sadness, for here we have to accept the reality that not all needs will be met on our terms. Not every want can be gratified at once and totally, if ever. There is disappointment as we face the fact that the world is not all 'good', and become willing to embrace and enjoy what is offered. For if the world is not perfectly responsive to our desires, neither is it all 'bad'. And what is true of our outer world is also true of the inner: we are neither sinless saints nor evil-hearted villains, though we have the capacity to behave like both.

But while growing older is inevitable, growing up is optional, and popular Western culture seems to shun maturity. It is simpler to live in a divided Kingdom, where some groups are 'in' and some are 'out'; where political spin by one party presents it as a roll-call of the righteous, while demonizing the actions and motives of the opposing camps; and where sports teams, celebrities and public figures endure reputations that flip between the pedestal and the gutter, with no intervening middle ground.

We can divide our individual world into separate states, according to our own personal definitions of 'good' and 'bad', and classify those we know as either friends or enemies, one of 'us' or one of 'them'.

We may also split our inner selves into 'good' and 'bad'. In Chapter 4 we noted that what we react against in others points to what we find hard to accept in ourselves. A human tendency is to separate such aspects off by 'projecting' them on to others, where they can be criticized freely. Thus we keep our halos brightly polished, but make others casualties in our own warring inner Kingdoms.

But persecuting others to keep ourselves pristine becomes increasingly burdensome and counterproductive. We end up living like latter-day King Canutes, ordering back the growing evidence of what we refuse to admit about ourselves. If we stand against this incoming tide in stubborn defiance, we are forced to try ever harder to defend our position against encroaching forces that beg to differ.

Protecting our preferred image of ourselves can ensnare us in unhealthy perfectionism, where nothing ever makes the grade, and achieving anything less than full marks effectively means we have failed. When nine people congratulate us on a task well done, but the tenth is critical, we compulsively diminish the nine and inflate the tenth response.

But when nothing is ever quite good enough, we sabotage opportunities for learning, change and growth. The full picture may fall short of our ideal, but midlife is a good time to have the courage to stop and look at it, rather than continue the struggle to keep up appearances.

The power of acceptance

By midlife, we have learned from experience that heavenly perfection can never be fully found among imperfect earthly circumstances. As one wise friend commented to my husband on changing jobs: 'Every new job is never as good as you hope nor as bad as you fear.'

What is true outwardly is also true within. Thus our first task in learning to live from inner reality rather than by outer roles is one of simple acceptance of all we find inside us, without picking and choosing. We cannot heal our inner divisions and move towards personal integration without acknowledging what needs to be reconciled. This does not mean endorsing anything and everything, but simply accepting its presence. Such a process usually involves a certain amount of disillusionment: the journey towards the depressive position may take us through difficult feelings before we come to clear-sighted peace about our whole selves.

Midlife can bring relationship and work upheavals. A change or loss of role can expose aspects of ourselves that we find unacceptable and threaten our underlying sense of identity.

> *Tamsin* felt rejected when her husband left her for another woman. Such feelings were compounded by her change of roles from wife to divorcee, and mother to single parent: 'I realized I had a set of assumptions about single parents and divorcees that made it very difficult to accept that those outer labels were now applied to me.'

Whether our clear categories of acceptability are being shaken from without or loosened from within, the process can make us feel that our lives are slipping out of our control. Far from bringing things together, such midlife experience can feel chaotic. We feel the vulnerability of being outside our personal comfort zone, even as we trust God to keep hold of all that seems to be falling apart.

But letting go of our efforts at self-protection, and allowing ourselves just to be, can ultimately bring relief as we learn to rest in the loving God who already knows and accepts everything contained in our inner being. We can become content to be on the journey, rather than having to prove we have arrived. It is a spiritual paradox that only by accepting the awkward can we truly move forward into something new.

The Christian gospel teaches us that we have been brought out of the dark into the light. As God's children we make a new beginning, but it is not long before we realize that though we have left the darkness, the darkness has not necessarily left us. It takes time to let go of old ways of doing things and grow into new patterns, as well as to realize that our greatest abilities can sometimes be our greatest liabilities.

The process itself is important, for it is only as we walk the Christian journey day by day that we develop a deeper relationship with God, and mature in character. When the Israelites arrived in the Promised Land, God did not allow them to occupy the whole land at once. It would have been too much to sustain. They needed to gain ground little by little.

Acceptance opens up the bigger picture, helps us to receive and offer a deeper compassion, brings both rest and renewed energy, and inspires awe at the mystery and complexity of God's creation. We may begin to see that:

- our greatest gifts can also harbour our darkest blind spots;
- our place of weakness is an opportunity for God's strength;
- all we have to offer is who we uniquely are;
- the quality of our relationships depends as much on who we are as who we are with;
- it is more valuable to aim for truth than strive for perfection;
- God's created world is as wonderful as it is wayward;
- the worst things in our lives can contain seeds of growth.

We are inclined to push away the unpalatable, fearful that otherwise it could push us over into discouragement. Yet Jesus himself declared that in this age, we have to reckon with a landscape that comprises both wheat and weeds alongside one another.

Taking responsibility

As we accept what we find growing within us at midlife, the second step is to take responsibility for who we are and what we have become. Some have wryly observed that this is not just true of what is on the inside: by the time we are 50, they say, the face, job and body we have is as much a matter of our own choices as our circumstances.

Jack found that his pattern of work followed a repeating cycle. At first, he was full of enthusiasm for the possibilities of his new employment, and saw his colleagues as congenial and supportive. But after a couple of years, he would feel differently:

yet again, he was not achieving his potential or gaining the recognition he deserved. Eventually, he would move on in search of a better job. A midlife redundancy forced him to face his work patterns and realize that underneath others' lack of recognition lay his own reserve and difficulties with believing in himself. Though he felt angry that others had not encouraged his career progression, Jack needed to take responsibility for his own manner and outlook.

At midlife it is finally time to 'own our projections', as we take responsibility for our whole selves. If we are giving another a hard time – perhaps a loved one or someone we perceive is in authority – and become aware that the real issue belongs to us, will we pull back and address it, rather than take things out on the other person? Will we dare to deal with the aspect of our own life that we would rather not admit to? Or will we avoid the challenge by diverting our energies into trying to control that very same aspect in someone else? Can we take responsibility for our emotions, and not say 'You made me feel bad' when we are the ones making ourselves feel that way?

Alongside reclaiming the responsibilities for ourselves that we might have inappropriately given away, midlife is also a time to review our responsibilities towards others. As members of the 'sandwich generation' (see Chapter 4), the balance of these may be shifting as our roles change in the family circle. New responsibilities may be emerging at one end of the generational spectrum while old responsibilities are having to be released at the other.

We may also need to acknowledge the limits of human responsibility. For example, while we can offer others emotional and practical support, we cannot ultimately be held accountable for their personal happiness. Even Jesus, who took on the responsibility of opening the way back to heaven for humankind by dying on our behalf, is not responsible for our decision to accept the route of redemption. In a culture eager to claim rights but reluctant to engage with responsibilities, it is perhaps particularly important that we seek God's wisdom and clarity about our areas of accountability (see Box 9).

Box 9   Reflecting on responsibilities

Here are some questions to ponder and apply to your different circles of family, work, church and community.

- What responsibilities do I take for others?
- What responsibilities do others take for me?
- What responsibilities do I take for myself?
- Am I avoiding a responsibility that belongs to me?
- Am I assuming a responsibility that belongs to another?
- Do I need to review and readjust some responsibilities in the light of changing roles?

Learning to negotiate

Amid the 'wheat and weeds' of midlife complexity in roles, responsibilities and relationships without and within, we can feel daunted at the prospect of sorting it all out. We realize now, if not before, that it is not always possible to solve the problem. We therefore need to adopt a more creative approach, directing our energies towards managing situations and resolving issues, rather than trying to rid ourselves of them. From this it follows that an essential midlife task is learning to negotiate.

We may feel a little wary about such an approach, especially if our upbringing at home or in church has predisposed us to see any accommodation of the other as spineless compromise. But when we seek to quell what threatens us rather than engage with it, we simply stir up its opposition, forcing us to fight harder or give up altogether (see Box 10).

The art of negotiation is not letting go of our 'essentials' but being willing to explore where each side can give way on some 'desirables' for the sake of finding a mutual meeting point. God in his holiness does not compromise on sin, but does seek to accommodate sinners. 'Come, let us reason together, says the Lord', reports the prophet Isaiah as God invites his people into a negotiation where he offers his forgiveness in exchange for their renewed obedience. Time and again, the God of glory chooses not to distance himself from our darkness

---

Box 10   Negotiation within

Daniel Levinson identified four key 'polarities' or opposites that need reworking at midlife. What do these mean to you? Are there other opposites you need to reconcile?[4]

Creation versus destruction
We have the capacity to be destructive as well as creative. How can we accept and harness that energy, to incorporate it into a richer creativity?

Masculine and feminine
Qualities more generally linked to our opposite gender may be seeking fuller expression. What outlets might we allow for such aspects, so that our personality becomes more whole?

Old versus young
Some parts of us are old (completed, declining, coming to fruition, weary); others are young (beginning, growing, full of possibilities, energetic). What do we need to let die and what do we need to nurture at this stage in our lives?

Attachment and separateness
Maturity brings an ability to separate. What connections have we released on our journey to independence? What meaningful attachments do we want to cultivate, now we are free of the compulsion of dependency?

---

but to redeem us; to work with what he has already made rather than start again with new material.

- God led his children into the Promised Land, despite the delay caused by their disobedience.
- God responded to David's penitence after the Bathsheba episode: he remained King, though he lost the child conceived in adultery.
- Jesus gave Peter a fresh start after he had denied his Lord in the courtyard.
- Jesus did not stone the woman caught in adultery but gave her a new chance, and exposed the darkness in the hearts of the outwardly holy and respectable Pharisees.[3]

Box 11   Jacob

Jacob was a quick-witted and forward-thinking schemer, with an eye for his own gain. He appropriated his brother Esau's birthright and fled for safety to the household of his uncle Laban in Haran. Over the next 20 years his abilities served him well as he acquired wives and wealth, proving himself more than a match for Laban.

A timely departure from Haran ultimately faced Jacob with the prospect of meeting his past in the form of his cheated brother Esau. Alone by the Jabbok river, with all the protective covering of his possessions and loved ones sent on ahead, the vulnerable Jacob encountered 'a man' who wrestled with him until dawn. It was a struggling with God himself, as human persistence met divine power. Jacob's tenacity won through: he received God's blessing as 'Israel', and his life was preserved. But his self-reliance was dealt a body-blow as God put his hip out of joint.

God brought Jacob into maturity through an engagement of opposites: Jacob the forward-planner was thrown into immediate physical reality; the one who thought himself in control was wrong-footed. Yet Jacob's energy was acknowledged and harnessed, not crushed in the process.

This divine rebalancing left Jacob physically weaker yet spiritually stronger, despite the fact that his walk was out of balance now he was left with a permanent limp. Yet he had a new name, and dependent Israel, limping home into his full inheritance in God's purposes, was stronger than entrepreneurial Jacob on the run.[5]

In our human relationships, without and within, we may find that honest acknowledgement of our position, and a willingness not to insist on having everything our own way, can enable us to turn what has been a dead-end into a place of possibilities for breaking through into new ground (see Box 11).

Yvonne's great potential at an early age gave her parents and teachers high hopes for her education. They wanted her to take an entrance exam for a prestigious private school rather than attend the local state school. But Yvonne did not want to leave all her friends. She acted in the only way she knew – by deliberately failing the exam. She had conformed outwardly but was inwardly rebellious.

By midlife, Yvonne began to realize this pattern had not stood her in good stead. She had used rebellion and walking out as a way of objecting to the expectations she felt others placed on her. This had lost her jobs and was now costing her a marriage.

She knew her rebellious streak was destructive but did not want to lose it. It gave her energy and made her feel powerful. Yvonne needed to find ways of giving this energy a more creative outlet: expressing her needs rather than acting them out; finding positive ways of being an individual instead of focusing resentfully on others' expectations; knowing when to use her energy to challenge and when simply to comply and co-operate.

Harry had loved being a youth worker. He loved the stimulus of being with young people, and gained huge satisfaction in seeing his contribution to their growth. But as midlife approached, he realized he did not have the stamina for the task as he used to, especially when his own family life seemed to be becoming more, rather than less, demanding. Harry did not want to admit it, but he was beginning to wonder whether he was outgrowing his usefulness in the role he had loved. Once he did confront the issue of whether his season of youth work had come to completion, he felt a great relief and freedom to consider other options.

Eventually, Harry became a trainer of other youth workers. No longer out in the field, but with a wealth of experience, he was able to fulfil his desire to nurture and develop younger lives in a different context. The freshness of this new challenge revitalized him.

The above situations reflect the need for negotiation both in our inner world and our outer circumstances, identifying a place of common ground rather than adopting a less mature, more primitive all-or-nothing stance. Such willingness to negotiate also meant that Yvonne and Harry could remain whole people: Yvonne did not have to suppress her rebellious energy to be an autonomous individual; Harry did not have to deny his ageing and changing circumstances. The midlife new balance-point is, as noted in Chapter 4, one of both/ and, not either/or.

The process of renegotiating with others or within ourselves is not always comfortable or easy; it can mean upheaval, relinquishment, disappointed expectations and a willingness to face the cost of change. We need to tackle the task with loving gentleness as well as fearless honesty.

Yet as we rise to the challenge of reappraising our roles and perhaps renegotiating them with those around us who are changing and growing, there is the potential for forging deeper relationships. As the midlife sandwich generation relates to those on either side, there is an opportunity to get to know our parents and children as real people while there is still time – an opportunity to be grasped and treasured.

Time to play

One final way of moving into a greater reality beneath our roles at midlife is to start expressing aspects of ourselves we may have previously avoided or disregarded but now find emerging and demanding our attention.

The arena where we can do this most creatively is that of re-creation. Here we can play with new approaches and activities, free of the pressures of expectation or achievement. The end of Chapter 4 indicated some possibilities for changing tastes and preferences that you might want to explore. Expressing new sides of ourselves, developing fresh skills or discovering new pleasures, is something we can do through play.

This, of course, is how a child learns. Play is a valuable and serious business, but by midlife the whole concept may have been largely left behind: play is for children, adulthood is about work. Yet while we may be called to let go of childishness, Jesus himself reminded us of the importance of having a child-like receptivity when it comes to the Kingdom of God.[6]

At midlife we may need to rediscover the place of play for relaxation, refreshment and release of our full role-free selves. It can be time to become more playful with what we have worked at so seriously, and to commit our best energies to what we have only played at up to now. By so doing we may come into a new balance, wholeness and depth of personality.

We cannot give away what we have not first received. At midlife we have the opportunity to accept ourselves, warts and all, in a deeper way. As we give our whole selves back to God who has made us and calls us, we find our offering gains a fuller and richer significance. But we also become aware that as our life's horizon broadens, it is also shortening.

Reflecting and responding

1 Reflect back over Levinson's four midlife 'polarities'. Are you aware of any other paired opposites within that you personally need to resolve, for example: rebel v. conformist, sociable v. private, stubborn v. flexible? How do they show themselves? How could they work effectively together rather than against one another?

Write or speak out what one side would say to the other. Now imagine what Jesus would say to each that would help negotiate reconciliation between them.

Follow this up with prayer by writing down your polarities on different pieces of paper and placing them by a Cross, as a way of offering your whole self to God. Reflect on how Jesus reconciled earth to heaven through the Cross. What parts of you might you need to die to, in order to live at peace with God, others and yourself?

2 Try doing an 'accountability audit' over one week to help you see clearly how you are managing your responsibilities. Use the questions from Box 9, Reflecting on Responsibilities, and add the word 'today' to each one. Record your answers to these questions at the end of each day for the next week. What patterns emerge? Are there some readjustments that need to be made as a result? How do you want to live the next seven days?

3 List the things in life that are work to you, and list the things that are play. How would it feel to swap the lists round and approach these activities differently? Are there some activities that involve both?

To explore this further, choose one work task, and consciously approach it in an attitude of play. As you perform it, adopt a lighter, carefree – though not careless – attitude. How does this affect the job in hand? Do you want to do any more radical rebalancing?

6

Facing our mortality

Plane journey

Take-off is no problem.
Racing engines roar,
Packed with power; eager for unleashing;
Gathering momentum and gaining speed.
Trepidation gives way to anticipation,
And the thrill of new horizons.
Then up, up into hospitable air,
Parting in gentleness to receive us,
And through the clouds, a Kingdom of possibilities opens out.

Landing is another matter.
No playful fall, but a disciplined descent,
Bringing loss of height and pace.
Vision is clouded over.
Options narrow to the dimensions of a runway,
And the reality of journey's end.
Now we bank for the final approach.
Tired minds concentrate to hold control of slackening engines,
And underneath, the ground, hard and uncompromising.

Julia McGuinness

When a man dies he clutches in his hand only that which he has given
away in his lifetime.

Jean Jacques Rousseau

Adjust to changing times, but cling to unchanging principles.

Jimmy Carter

I cannot become holy by following another's path . . . I have to take
my own steps, and create a life that has never been lived before.

Rowan Williams

So teach us to count our days
that we may gain a wise heart.
Psalm 90.12

The reality of mortality

Bill was a frustrating fellow student. He turned out magnificent essays with effortless creativity while the rest of us toiled for hours in the library. A real 'character', Bill was a gregarious, warm-hearted Christian, with a lively sense of humour. He was instantly recognizable by his trademark never-washed Arran jumper, spectacles repaired by Sellotape, and dark tousled hair. After graduating, Bill established himself as a gifted and versatile writer. One aspect of his work was travel writing. In 1992, Bill was on a Thai Airways flight to Kathmandu to research his next book, when his plane crashed headlong into the Nepalese mountainside. There were no survivors. Bill was 34 years old.[1]

As Bill's contemporary, I felt his death profoundly: death was no longer the preserve of the elderly, but could happen within my own generation – even to me.

The psychoanalyst Elliott Jaques, who is credited with coining the phrase 'mid-life crisis', saw the realization of personal mortality as its key marker. He felt this happened towards the end of one's thirties. While individual circumstances and experience mean that this stage cannot be so precisely dated, there is a truth in his observation. As Jaques says, 'The paradox is that of entering the prime of life, the stage of fulfilment, but at the same time the prime and fulfilment are dated. Death lies beyond.'[2]

Western secular culture is significantly death-avoidant, and conspires to shield us from the mortal truth. The hospice movement has done much to combat the terror and mystery of dying, but this still means that death generally happens away from home. Death is reported as an unfortunate occurrence rather than the common experience. We read that someone 'lost their battle with cancer', as if the ultimate outcome was ever in doubt.

Whatever our earlier bereavements, midlife is often the first time death comes up close and personal. Many will be facing, in reality or in prospect, a parental death, and the rise in the mortality rate in the 45–60 age range increases the likelihood of our experiencing the premature death of someone in our circle through illness, accident or worse.

We may already 'know' our mortality intellectually, but when we fully absorb it emotionally it can make a powerful impact. Alongside feeling their own vulnerability, some experience deep anxiety about how loved ones would fare without them. At midlife our responsibilities and relationship networks are in their prime. But even letting go of the illusion that we are indestructible can leave us clinging on to the one that says we are indispensable.

Life's endings

Death may be the end of our time in this world, but our life's course takes us through many endings. Margaret Guenther comments on our mortality that, 'we live with our own small reminders, our own "last things".'[3] How we manage such losses and completions on our way is an indicator of what we will bring to our ultimate ending.

How do we respond to endings? Do we prefer not to talk about them, or 'cut and run' prematurely to avoid the actual pain of parting? Do we prolong our involvement in some area of life rather than let go of a responsibility or activity? Do we plan for endings or prefer not to think about what is coming next? How do we manage unfinished business? Do we anticipate a certain amount of satisfaction and relief, or fear regret and loss?

However we have answered, our initial reaction does not have to be our final response. We all bring our own personal baggage of experience and coping mechanisms when it comes to facing loss, but life's 'last things' offer opportunities to process and mature our approach. At the midlife point we trust we still have many lesser endings to come, before our final curtain. There is time to prepare for the inevitable; to learn to end well.

But what characterizes a good ending? Below are some suggestions.

- The ending is faced openly.
- The ending is prepared for.
- Unfinished business has been addressed.
- What needs to be said has been spoken (or written): words of love, gratitude, forgiveness, parting.
- There is due consideration and preparation given to successors.
- There is an appropriateness and completeness in the timing.
- There is a legacy to celebrate, a contribution to be remembered.
- There is a letting go, a grieving and an acceptance of ending on all sides.

Though ending brings loss, this is not necessarily connected with decay or failure. A good ending carries within it a sense of completion. Jesus' dying words on the Cross were: 'It is finished.' Paul writes to Timothy of his own impending death as marking the end of his life's race, where he has kept the faith to the finishing line.[4] Yet not all endings are experienced as timely fulfilment.

> *Linda* was shaken to the core as the revelation of her husband's infidelity led to the painful ending of her marriage. Yet for her this trauma exposed an even more disturbing reality: 'It made me realize there were things in life I had absolutely no control over. In the long term this actually distressed me as much as the marriage breakdown itself.'

An unwelcome and unexpected ending threatens our security and dispels any illusion of invincibility. Linda was brought up sharp, the foundations of her Christian faith and life shaken. Only with time, perseverance and loving support, was she able to turn towards God rather than away from him, and choose to trust her personal vulnerability into his hands.

The shock of a premature death, such as Bill's, cuts brutally across our sense of a natural God-given rhythm of life and death. Yet we live in a fallen world. And while Jesus fulfilled his Father's purpose, even his redemptive work did not include a full earthly lifespan as he became a fully vulnerable human being.

Where life seems cut short for no discernible good purpose, we can only look to the Psalmist's prayer for comfort, if not understanding: 'In your book were written all the days that were formed for me, when none of them as yet existed.'[5]

When ending rides roughshod over completion, we need to ask God to work completion within us from our side; to soothe our raw edges and minister to our loose ends; to bring an acceptance of what we cannot change because it is beyond our control. Ultimately we need to trust the one who can make the desert bloom to bring something beautiful even out of grief's barrenness, so we regain the Christian hope that 'all things work together for good for those who love God, who are called according to his purpose'.[6]

What we leave behind

The shock of another's untimely ending brings the realization that ultimately we have no guarantees about our own lifespan. The New Testament writers regularly exhorted their Christian readers to live in readiness for the life to come. Their sense of the imminent Second Coming of Christ went alongside the call to be ready for one's own personal 'day of the Lord'.

There is a practical dimension to being prepared to leave this life: midlife, if not before, is a time when many choose to make a will – though it is estimated that currently 60 per cent of the UK population has not done so. It may feel like a contingency plan, but we are aware that death is a real contingency.

A more immediate matter that may bring things uncomfortably closer to home is considering our own funeral arrangements. Christianne Heal, co-founder of the Natural Death Centre, observes that most people put great effort into organizing occasions such as weddings and baptisms, so why not funerals?[7] Such forward thinking, preferably talked through, but certainly written down for loved ones, can spare those grieving the additional responsibility of trying to decide what the departed would have wished for their funeral.

But awareness of our death raises issues beyond material provision and funeral planning. It urges us to focus on our legacy in a much deeper sense. Have we offered our unique contribution to making a positive difference to those around us? Will we leave the world a better place for those who follow on? However impressive our

---

Box 12 Time well spent?

● If you are able, look at your appointments diary and/or journal for the last year. What has claimed your attention, time and energy?
● If you knew that this was to be your last year, would you have used it in the same way? If not, sketch out what you would have put into the diary – remembering that would mean taking some things out!
● What is it important to make space for in the year ahead?

---

achievements, what is their long-term significance? Jesus said: 'For what will it profit them to gain the whole world but forfeit their life?' This becomes profoundly relevant as we reflect on what is of ultimate value (see Box 12).

Facing our mortality sensitizes us to our life's purpose: being prepared for what is to come has implications for how we are living now. Death's quiet whisper in our ear, through whatever circumstances or experiences it comes, sounds as a sharp wake-up call to act on those changes we otherwise never quite get round to making – from seeking reconciliation to losing weight. Knowing our stay in this world is time-limited can result in big shifts in outlook and even occupation. It is the urgency of 'If not now, when?'

Nigel worked in heavy industry. One day he finished a conversation with a workmate and went for his coffee break. He came back to find his workmate fatally injured by a piece of industrial machinery. After his initial shock and grief, this incident eventually led to a profound change in Nigel's working life. He left his manufacturing job to work on an environmental project. It meant earning less, but he knew that if time was limited, he wanted to do something that ultimately meant more to him.

Identifying what holds this meaning for us raises other questions. In longing for something of ourselves and our contribution to this world to live on, we are looking at what is valuable beyond our generation. We are expressing a hunger in our hearts for eternity; we are beginning to consider spiritual issues.

What we face ahead

Consciousness of death calls us to face the reality of our relationship with God and our faith in the life to come. This factor amid the other issues of transition may make midlife a season of spiritual upheaval too.

We may start questioning the old, taught certainties of our younger Christian lives. In Chapter 4 we looked at the challenge to grow beyond a black/white approach to ourselves and others, and this may include our relationship with God. Life-experience can stretch our spiritual life to breaking point as we try to hold to our image of God's goodness through the dark filters of adversity or unanswered prayer.

Faced with his apparent unresponsiveness when we cry out may lead some to write off the Almighty as a 'bad', or non-existent, God in their eyes. Others resolve the conundrum by concluding that they must be 'bad' Christians – or at least deficient in faith. Too many Christians struggling with a situation of ongoing hurt know the experience of being approached by well-meaning believers armed with *the* Bible verse to name and claim for assured results. But bludgeoning the Almighty with Scripture and screwing up our faith muscles to force his hand is no fail-safe formula for achieving our heart's desire.

Midlife honesty compels us to admit that things are not so simple. It acknowledges the stark reality that Christianity offers no guaranteed magical fixes for life's problems. Our own assumptions and expectations are up for scrutiny, as the blanket faith statements that once satisfied us no longer pacify our inner disquiet.

We may also feel caught up in living out a Christian role, but wondering about the reality of our relationship with God beneath. Perhaps we sense we have assigned God a role in our lives as the immediate provider of our wants and protector of our interests – a role we cannot make him fit any more – see Box 13 (overleaf).

Midlife raises many uncomfortable questions, yet the very time when we need to draw more deeply on our faith's foundations can

---

Box 13   Changing faith; unchanging God

God does not change but we do. Look at the list below and reflect on
how you would have understood and engaged with them 20 years ago
(and/or when you first professed a Christian faith) and how you understand and engage with them today. What has changed, and why? How
do you regard these changes?

Father, Son and Holy Spirit	Second Coming
Sin	The Bible
Born-again	Healing
Prayer	Spiritual gifts
Church	Eternal life
Holy Communion	Evangelism
Creation	Heaven and hell

---

be when we find that the familiar styles of prayer, worship, doing
church and Christian living, start going stale on us. What used to work
loses its lustre, leaving some anxious that they are losing their faith
altogether.

As different aspects of our personality emerge and tastes and preferences shift, this naturally has a disorientating effect on our spiritual life, yet our concerns can be hard to voice, given the almost
unconscious conspiracy of silent conformity existing in some church
fellowships. Some midlife believers become spiritually isolated as
they carry on pretending. Rather than dare to break ranks, they cling
to hopes that somehow the inner dis-ease will go away.

A more creative response is to use this discontent with going through
the motions as the springboard to search for a more meaningful
Christian way of being. Since midlife brings a pressing need for our
faith-journey to be personally authentic, this quest will involve a certain element of 'aloneness'.

Such a journey calls for courage, but discovering a route to a
deeper and richer level of faith means daring to venture out into
unknown territory. Indeed, it could be argued that every spiritual
breakthrough requires some disorientation and darkness on the
way, as past comfort zones are surrendered: resurrection can only be
preceded by death.

It also takes time and patience. It is not uncommon for Christians to go through a midlife 'wilderness', a season that can last months, perhaps years. Gone are the youthful days when a spiritual crisis could be resolved by a late-night coffee and prayer with a friend.

Christian midlife transition involves questioning received certainties, old structures and set patterns. Christianity comprises a core of non-negotiable tenets of faith. At midlife we realize how additional habits, practices and assumptions may gradually have attached themselves to underlying truths, like barnacles to the hull of a ship. Our task is to discern what needs to be scraped away and what needs to be maintained and cherished, so our voyage of faith is not hampered as we travel into uncharted waters ahead.

Carl Jung observed that whatever the presenting problem of the two-thirds of his patients who were in the second half of life, the underlying issue was a spiritual one. So it should not surprise us that while some midlifers are re-evaluating their lives from the position of a practising faith, others are finding faith for the first time.

Tim discarded a Catholic upbringing where he was 'dragged to church', but experienced a personal crisis in his forties. His work as a paramedic went through a particularly traumatic period: 'I had a string of bad jobs, and it knocked me sideways.'

Though he was now in a supportive second marriage, Tim needed time off and counselling support. At one point, his counsellor asked, 'What do you think will happen to you when you die?' Mindful of his earlier divorce, Tim found himself saying, 'I think I'll burn in hell.'

On the counsellor's suggestion, Tim attended the Alpha course that transformed his life.

'I had a powerful experience of God's forgiveness and felt completely different. I thought: "What have I been missing all these years?" Something has really grown inside me. I only wish it had happened earlier.'

Tim's midlife conversion has brought a surge of energy that he has directed into Christian outreach activities: 'I feel Jesus has given me another chance, and I want to use it. I feel very strongly about what's happened to me. I'll tell anyone about it.'

Claire worshipped in an evangelical charismatic fellowship throughout her early adulthood. Her midlife Christian journey began when she was faced with a Christian leader who seemed to see issues of faith in very black/white terms.

'I wanted to say, "How do you know you're right?", and that made me think, "How do I know I'm right?"'

Claire's subsequent explorations shifted her understanding of many aspects of her Christian faith and practice. She now belongs to an Anglo-Catholic church.

'I see my path as a journey towards God. For me, the central truth is that God is love. My faith is as real as it ever was, but now it's more thought-out and informed. I've grappled with doubt and come out the other side.'

Tim's journey to faith led to him joining church; Claire's resulted in her changing church. The course of a midlife spiritual journey may involve moving to a different worshipping community, but this is not an option to take lightly. If we are disillusioned with 'church' it can be tempting to cut and run, either isolating ourselves from the Christian body or joining what we hope will be the perfect church, only to find our expectations disappointed.

We need to be honest with ourselves: simply rearranging the Christian furniture will not solve the problems we are carrying inside us. However, there may come a point when we feel utterly stuck in a setting where we can neither contribute positively nor grow spiritually. In such a situation, we need to reflect prayerfully on where we are called to belong.

The issue of mortality can sometimes help resolve the matter. Asking the question, 'Is this the church where I would like my funeral?' can be a great clarifier, as it reveals the strength of attachment to our current spiritual home. How content we are for this to be the place where we complete our life's Christian journey will expose any need for significant change, internal or external.

Leaving a church always needs to be done graciously, as does letting go of any ministry or long-standing church role. How we leave

---

Box 14   An alphabet of maturing Christian spirituality in midlife and beyond

- Acceptance of ambiguity
- 'Being' as important as 'doing'
- Clarity about our call
- Detachment from driven-ness
- Eagerness to experiment
- Freedom to fail
- Groundedness in God's grace
- Humility and honesty about our humanity
- Integration of our shadow and 'negative' emotions
- Journeying and journalling
- Kindness towards others and self
- Less listing, more listening in prayer
- Movement from magic to mystery
- Nurture of our inner life
- Ordinary living is a place of divine encounter
- Playfulness as well as profundity
- Questioning and questing
- Rhythm of work and rest
- Solitude and space
- Trust in God's timing
- Uncluttering of lifestyle
- Valuing of family and friends
- Wisdom and waiting
- X-Factor – openness to the unknown
- Yearning to be authentic rather than perfect
- Zest for the present moment

---

is as important as whether we leave a Christian fellowship. It should never be too easy to say goodbye.

Yet staying within our particular fellowship may also be a creative choice. As we journey through midlife transition and become more personally grounded in the essentials of our faith, our relationship with our church community is likely to change: to involvement without dependency; to detachment without aloofness; to acceptance without compromise; and to contributing out of calling not compulsion – see Box 14.

Receiving the present

Earlier we noted that the midlife view of the future is of limited time remaining rather than an endlessly expanding horizon. If quantity is limited, then quality has to count.

One benefit of a time-limited counselling contract is how it encourages important issues to be faced rather than allowed to run on. What is not in endless supply is used more effectively.

The same can apply to the time-limited contract of our lifespan – though we do not have access to the small print to know just how long our life here is to be.

Becoming conscious of our mortality may pull us up short at first, but facing the reality of our own death can ultimately prove life-enhancing. We truly make more of each day, knowing it is finite. By embracing our ending we are free to embrace our living more fearlessly. The great gift of midlife awareness of mortality is a deeper appreciation of the present moment as ultimately all we have.

David Watson's account of his own journey with cancer quotes a director of radiography's striking observation that the illness 'makes people start thinking about the quality of their lives. Everything they do has a keener edge to it and they get more out of life. In fact, some people never become completely human beings until they get cancer.'[8]

But we do not have to wait for illness to cherish life more fully. Those who have meditated on their mortality report it as a liberating experience, intensifying their appetite for life and sharpening their focus on what really matters. In such meditation, we find our priorities fall naturally into order: we know deep down what is important to us, but often do not take time to connect with it.

As we make that connection in the present, we start to face the future with renewed confidence and clarity. It is to that looking ahead that we now turn.

Reflecting and responding

1 Reflect on the different endings you have experienced in life. Which have had the greatest significance for you? How have you dealt with them? Does a pattern emerge? Are there any endings you want to revisit or complete as a result?

2 Write your own epitaph. How would you like to be remembered? What would you like to be remembered for? Are you living in a way now that would make this epitaph something that another would write on your behalf? If not, what needs to change?

3 Plan your funeral service. Where would you like to be buried/cremated/have ashes scattered? What could you write down and let people know about that would help them follow your wishes if you were to die unexpectedly? This includes making a will if you have not already done so.[9]

4 Give yourself some quiet space and write two headings on a blank sheet of paper:

'If I died tonight I would be grateful for . . .'
'If I died tonight I would regret . . .'

List things under these headings and spend some time in thanksgiving prayers for items in the first column. Think about how you might express your appreciation and gratitude to those whom you have named in your prayers.

Ask the Holy Spirit to give you some guidance as to how to address the issues in the second column. Not everything can change at once, but you may wish to make some changes in the light of what emerges. Has anything of what you have written surprised you?

5 Below are some widely regarded elements of a practised Christian faith. Which of these are negotiables and which are essentials to you?

- A conversion experience
- A daily quiet time each morning
- Church worship on Sunday
- Speaking in tongues
- Singing choruses and/or traditional hymns

- Care for the environment
- Tithing at ten per cent
- Keeping the Sabbath
- Saving sex for marriage
- No remarriage of divorcees
- Abstaining from alcohol and cigarettes
- Not participating in lotteries, raffles, sweepstakes, etc.

7

Renewing our hope

Back on track

It wasn't just water from the pool that had refreshed him, thought the Traveller as he resumed his journey through the forest. He felt quite a different person from the one who had sat heavily down that day, weary and wondering if it was worth continuing the expedition. His surroundings, now suffused by the tawny light of autumn sunshine, had certainly lost their springtime freshness. Yet the Traveller was surprised at how renewed he felt after his 'time out'. What had changed?

Perhaps it was that he was carrying less as he set off this time. This had seemed unnatural at first. As the Traveller walked away from the clearing, his steps had felt heavy. He was tempted to turn back to pick up the things he was leaving behind, but he resisted and kept his eyes ahead. After a while, he found himself enjoying the lightness of his pack rather than mourning the loss of its contents.

Perhaps it was that he had settled on his direction. The Traveller had become overwhelmed by so many paths and possibilities in the forest. Consulting his original map hadn't helped, criss-crossed and covered as it was with others' advice about different routes. It was only in sorting through his pack that he rediscovered his compass and Traveller's Guide. Now he'd decided to rely on these instead. Setting a simple compass direction brought a sense of freedom and focus that settled any dilemmas about the detail. And the Guide was teaching him how to travel rather than where to go.

Perhaps it was that he was noticing so much more around him, now that these issues were resolved: the birdsong; tiny flowers in the glades; the forest creatures.

Despite his energy, the Traveller knew he was not covering ground as fast as he had once done. He had a less precise idea of his destination, yet somehow more confidence in the direction of his journey.

And he felt a renewed sense of anticipation at the discoveries he might make on the way.

Julia McGuinness

Change has the power to uplift, to heal, to stimulate, surprise, open new doors, bring fresh experiences and create excitement in life. Certainly it is worth the risk.

Leo Buscaglia

Somewhere along the line of development we discover what we really are, and then we make our real decision for which we are responsible. Make that decision primarily for yourself because you can never really live anyone else's life, not even your own child's. The influence you exert is through your own life and what you become yourself.

Eleanor Roosevelt

Do not remember the former things,
or consider the things of old.
I am about to do a new thing;
now it springs forth, do you not perceive it?
I will make a way in the wilderness
and rivers in the desert.

Isaiah 43.18, 19

Turning points

'Perhaps most people go through a period of midlife dissatisfaction,' mused a friend one evening over a glass of wine. 'But few can do anything radical about it. So they just find a way of living through it until eventually the difficult feelings go away.'

Stoically battening down the hatches when midlife disturbance descends can seem tempting, but in the long term this can lead to rigidity and stagnation.

It is never easy to experience restless feelings, and midlife is no exception. Yet such discomforting upheaval comes as a gift, calling us to reappraise our way of living and make appropriate adjustments.

The Greek word 'crisis' is linked to the verb 'krinein'. This carries within it various shades of meaning incorporating 'to separate, judge or decide'. A midlife crisis prompts us to look more discerningly at our past and choose from within our present circumstances how we intend to invest our energies in the future.

We are likely to want to make some creative changes. 'Life', as the writer Derek Milne observes, 'is too short for more of the same',[1] and by midlife we may well be losing the will to live in the same old way, doing the same old things at the same old pace.

Change involves a certain amount of effort, however we want to rebalance our lifestyle or reorientate our activities. Yet if we choose wisely, we will eventually reap the benefits in regained momentum and renewed spirits. The energy pouring down the drain of defending our old patch will be redirected into a more life-enhancing course. This will carry us onward into life's next phase with a new zest. Change is not just an option at midlife; it is essential for personal growth.

We have considered how a midlife awareness of mortality can urge us to engage more fully with life now. Indeed, some regard midlife transition as primarily about life per se. The psychologist George Vaillant sees midlife pain as 'preparatory to entering a new stage of man' (*sic*). He dismisses concern with death in favour of the birth of a 'second adulthood'.[2]

Carl Jung acknowledges life's mid-point as an end-point for particular ways of living, but he also sees the transition more in terms of womb than tomb. Midlife upheaval signifies a person's birth-anxiety about who they are becoming, rather than fear of future ending.

The paradox is that both views apply. As another psychologist, William Bridges, notes, a midlife acceptance of what will now never be 'can sometimes open the door to new activities and new achievements that were impossible under the old dreams'.[3]

The Christian hope of resurrection gives people of faith particular insight into the overlap between womb and tomb: both are places of darkness and hidden inner space from which God brings forth new life into the light at the appointed time. We might even see Lazarus, entombed for four days before being summoned back to life by Jesus, as the one with the most profound experience of 'second adulthood' in history![4]

We may feel like a midlife Lazarus, bound up in the grave-clothes of past choices and trapped in the tomb of present circumstances, but God is in the business of bringing life out of death. As we make peace with our past and reckon with present realities, Jesus' voice calls us to journey on towards the light.

Regaining a new vision in due season is vital. Jesus cautioned his would-be disciples that those called to plough a new furrow who looked back were not Kingdom material. And in the Old Testament, God commanded Lot and his family not to turn round as they fled Sodom's destruction. We can damage ourselves through over-preoccupation with where we have come from, as Lot's wife found out to her cost when she looked behind her and came to a salty standstill.[5]

Amid the doldrums of midlife the prospect of moving on seems daunting, yet Lazarus came to life in response to Jesus' call. By stopping to listen and question ourselves, we will be more attuned to his still small voice, clarifying our direction and putting us in touch with what he has made us for.

Reclaiming our passion

God-given passion, used creatively, empowers and enables. Through it, the terminally ill live past their prognosis; society's carers and campaigners for justice persevere against the odds; the poor and disadvantaged succeed beyond expectation; faithful partners sustain love over a lifetime.

Such passion has fuelled humankind's noblest actions, highest achievements, finest hours, most creative artistry and richest discoveries. It is no passing infatuation, thoughtless frenzy or distorted self-serving, but a deep-seated emotion of the heart that can override personal convenience for the sake of its goal. It is no coincidence that passion is the word used to describe Christ's pathway to the Cross.

At midlife, we may have become used to hiding our passions, even from ourselves, perhaps out of deference to others' expectations or for the sake of outward control. These dormant desires represent aspects of ourselves that God has created but are yet to come fully to life, and they contain a great source of untapped energy. Recognizing and

---

Box 15   The inward connection

- What were the day-dreams of my youth?
- What have I always wanted to do but never dared to try?
- What do I really want to do?
- Who do I really want to be?
- What gets in the way?

---

releasing them is a key to allowing God to resource us through midlife and beyond.

We may have a deep yearning for a particular experience – a visit to a special place, trip to the opera, ride in a hot-air balloon – but other desires can also rumble under the surface. Perhaps you harbour a longing to learn a particular skill, take up a hobby, write children's stories, run a marathon, organize a local carnival or create a small garden. At midlife we need to unearth our buried passions and find ways of putting them to work. 'If not now, when?'

This is not selfishness, but the appropriate self-expression of our God-createdness. It is not about achieving targets but about letting live what God has put within. A divinely directed passion always enriches or makes whole in some way, even if it simply revitalizes us to engage our existing responsibilities in life with fresh vigour and vision. Wherever our passion is located, welcoming it into the open can help break the grip of midlife 'stuckness' and rekindle hope (see Box 15).

Realizing our purpose

True God-given passion takes us beyond ourselves. Perhaps that is why we can be reluctant to let it out. Like Pandora's box, we do not know quite what we are unleashing or where it will take us. Yet there are also consequences to sitting on the box-lid. At midlife we face the choice of closing in on ourselves or opening out – of moving towards self-centredness or self-transcendence.

Paul reminds the Ephesians that as Christians we are, 'created in Christ Jesus for good works, which God prepared beforehand to be our way of life'.[6] Part of that preparation is his placing within us a desire to do these works as an outflowing of who we are. So eliciting our God-endowed passion will ultimately direct us towards the unique purpose he has placed at the heart of our being.

At midlife, the value of what we devote ourselves to becomes a more pressing concern. Reconnecting with what stirs our hearts to active involvement can revitalize us to move into life's second half creatively and confidently. William Bridges poignantly observes that, 'Carried free of the old conflicts and confusions of trying to make it, and carried out into the clear water of self-knowledge and service, many people find at last what they were meant to do and be.'[7]

We will know our God-endowed passion by its various characteristics:

- its emphasis is creative rather than productive;
- it is personal – owned from within, not imposed from outside;
- it brings blessing or benefit to others in some way;
- it is challenging and demands our concentration;
- it brings out the best in us;
- it is absorbing – we can lose track of time when we are involved in it;
- it results in something of lasting value;
- it can make a positive difference;
- ultimately it sustains rather than drains us.

As we ask ourselves some searching questions, we may find that reconnecting with our deepest desires brings bigger implications than simply setting aside an evening a week or planning a one-off expedition. We may be challenged to re-direct our whole way of life if we are to live true to our ultimate Christian calling. Big changes can result: the journalist becomes a teacher; the teacher becomes a writer; the finance director retrains as a psychotherapist; the full-time mother founds a charity.

One of the devil's dissuaders to midlifers is the discouraging whisper of, 'Why bother? You're too old', or 'It's too late'. Yet even if we only have limited years left to pursue our new course, it is still worth going for it.

The culmination of Jesus' incarnation was a radical career change from carpenter to itinerant preacher and healer as he proclaimed

---

Box 16   Janine

Janine's flair for organization made her an effective worker in financial administration before she left to have her first baby. Becoming a mother drew forth her marked nurturing gifts. As these interwove with her organizational skills, Janine found herself running the church crèche, and then a Sunday school class. As her children grew, she discovered she did not want to return to finance, but to retrain as a primary school teacher. At 40, she qualified with flying colours and began working full-time. Despite its demands, she brings an enthusiasm to her teaching that reflects a sustaining midlife passion and the discovery of a true vocation at the right time.

God's coming Kingdom. Given the life-expectancy of a first-century Palestinian male, this could perhaps be seen as a midlife change of direction. This season of Jesus' ministry lasted a mere three years or so, yet eternal blessing has flowed from such a fleeting period.

If we fail to respond to the challenge of 'If not now, when?' we risk the later regret of, 'If only . . .' An observation by the psychological writer Dennis Bromley is salutary: 'We may grossly overrate ourselves and fail to appreciate the limited freedom we have to control our own fate', but 'we may underrate ourselves and never discover what we could have become.'[8]

The worldly 'wisdom' that views old as obsolete can distort our view of the 'foolishness' of God's time scales. God's purposes encompass our whole lifespan. The crime novelist P. D. James, who began her writing career in her late thirties, has observed that it can be too early to start an enterprise, as well as too late. Certain experience and accumulated wisdom may be necessary precedents to our particular call (see Box 16), and Scripture bears witness to the fact that age is no barrier to God doing a new thing, bringing to life an old one or leading us into a vocation whose time has now come.

If letting God bring to life a long-harboured passion brings the bittersweet feeling of wishing we had acted before, we need to remember that what matters is our obedience in the present. The best time to plant a tree may be 20 years ago, but the second-best time is now.

Box 17 The upward call

- What activities do I get so caught up in that I lose myself?
- What represents the deepest and best within me?
- What are the unique gifts that I alone can contribute?
- What energizes, inspires and calls me?
- Where might it take me?

While discerning a God-given passion may mean revolution for some, others may feel a sense of resolution. They find themselves finally aware of the underlying motivation for what they have already been drawn to do in life: the artist may become conscious of a deep call to communicate; the caterer, of a heart to bring people together through providing sustenance; the builder, of a vocation to create something serviceable that will last.

Seeing the connectedness between the disparate threads of our life-story can be liberating and energizing in itself, as it has been for a doctor who left work to care for her children full-time. Only in looking back did she fully see how her desire to nurture people to wholeness had fuelled her activities in both settings.

Whether identifying our God-given passion means midlife redirection or readjustment, either way a fresh sense of purpose can revitalize our journey (see Box 17).

Re-appraising our priorities

'I'm getting to the stage where I want to do a few things, and do them well,' said a prominent Christian speaker approaching his fiftieth birthday. Once we have identified our passion and clarified our purpose, we need to set some priorities if we are to live out their implications. From redirecting to readjusting our path, midlife brings the urge to simplify our lifestyle, cutting out any clutter that fuzzes the focus of what now matters most.

Accumulation is the emphasis of youth: growth means increase, and progress is signified by achievement. At midlife we reach the

---

Box 18   The onward path

- What are the things in my life that I want to put first?
- Where am I living by the clock rather than the compass?
- What are the tension points between what I should do, what I desire to do and what I end up doing?
- How can I make the time to do what really matters most?

---

stage of maturation, as we realize that more and higher does not always mean better. Jesus' parable of the vine that needs pruning to be fully fruitful can be a threatening concept to a young Christian. Deliberately cutting back healthy growth is hard to take on board emotionally. But midlife brings deeper insight into the maxim that the good can be the enemy of the best. We can dare to lose some grapes – or perhaps whole branches – for the sake of a richer wine: the ability to act is not the same as the call to do.

Midlife prioritizing involves realism about our pace of activity as well as its range. As another Christian minister commented, 'I have to accept that I cannot do at 45 what I could at 35.' A drive for achieving speed needs to give way to a call to sustaining stamina – life is a marathon, not a sprint. A compulsion to quantity needs to be replaced by a commitment to quality – life is a workshop, not a production line (see Box 18).

Such changes affect our whole way of operating, and their impact is bound to be felt by those around us. Some may be disappointed that we can no longer perform at their pace, or do all they have come to expect. Others may be delighted that we are somehow more 'present' to them. Some may be shocked at our change of occupation, particularly if it means stopping something we were perceived to be doing well; others may be struck by a sense of deeper well-being emanating from us as we live with greater personal integrity.

At midlife, as never before, it is the time to stop wearing ourselves out for others' agendas, and start living according to our call and for others' blessing.

Choice and limitation

Setting our priorities faces us with an inherent midlife tension, which the Jungian analyst Murray Stein summarizes as, 'the conviction of a future life-task' running alongside 'the knowledge of limits'.[9]

Learning to hold this two-fold awareness and find a balance-point that incorporates both elements is the creative way' through choppy waters of midlife disturbance towards the calm pool of renewed, maturing adulthood.

Working towards this resolution will involve serious reflection and exploration. It will demand a fearless personal honesty and a dispassionate look at our life situation.

There are real issues at stake. For example, if we do change our main occupation, we are unlikely to have the career prospects that would once have opened up for us. Yet if our focus is now on vocation rather than personal advancement, this may feel less important.

Perhaps more pertinent are the material implications a new course holds for ourselves and our dependants: an employed parent may feel trapped by being a breadwinner. Yet a home-making parent may feel equally trapped by domestic responsibilities. Moreover, a parent who has stayed at home for a lengthy period may also struggle with self-confidence in going back out to work. It is vital not to devalue personal abilities, skills and experience in the domestic setting compared to the more widely recognized qualifications of the market place.

Finding the balance between life-task and limitation may not involve total career change. Other options could be part-time or portfolio working; reducing employed hours to release space for relationships, other interests and overall well-being; fewer formal meetings, more community involvement; moving house or area; changing church or ministry; a simpler lifestyle, with less spending and doing; widening or deepening one's social circle; more space for solitude, reflection and creativity.

At midlife we may feel overwhelmed by changes we can do nothing about – from our ageing bodies, growing families and changing roles, to technological advance and global warming. At such times we can slip back into black/white, either/or thinking. Assuming that if we cannot do everything, there is no point in doing anything, we write off the possibility of change.

But we always have some choices. By exercising our freedom, at whatever level, we dispel the feeling of powerlessness that can intensify midlife transition into a crisis. It is not that we are in total control of life. At midlife we finally lose the illusion that we are ultimately in control of anything. But we do take back the authority God gives us over our circumstances to respond to him actively in every situation.

Lazarus was brought back to life to enjoy a renewed adulthood, despite his decaying body. What did that resurrection mean for the remainder of his earthly days? What decomposing dreams might God want to draw us out of into the light of a new living hope?

When God places boundary stones around our lives, we are commanded not to move them. But some stones are obstacles to be challenged and overcome. Box 19 (overleaf) offers some questions to ask about the rock that may lie across your Christian path.

Even if we experience all our circumstances and previous choices as immovable, we are still not trapped: we can ask God to meet us where we are and change our outlook, so that we can say with the Psalmist: 'The boundary lines have fallen for me in pleasant places; I have a goodly heritage.'[10]

Paul urges us to 'be transformed by the renewing of your minds'.[11] Part of the midlife process is to transform our view of what we have and who we are now, wherever we have come to. Indeed, gaining a fresh perspective is an absolute necessity in finding a creative way forward regardless of our life-situation.

If reconnecting with our midlife passion has recalled us to why we chose our particular life-path, we may still need to recapture our original vision, to re-energize us for the way ahead.

The Christian writer Joyce Rupp experienced this as she faced midlife doubt about vows she made when joining her religious community a quarter of a century earlier. She came to realize that the unchanging values behind her vows of celibacy, poverty and obedience could continue with enriched significance if seen as commitments to compassion, simplicity and community. This positive

---

Box 19 Reading the rocks

Can you move it?
God can provide the resources to shift some obstacles. Ask for the strength to move it, or for the power of God to move the mountain in response to your prayer.

Can you step over it?
Sometimes God uses the very obstacle itself as a stepping stone for his purposes. Paul's Jewish background became a bridge, not a bar, to his call to Christian mission.

Can you go round it?
Perhaps God would guide you to his destination via another route. Reflect on how this happened to the Holy Family and the Magi in the Nativity story.

Can you carry it?
Perhaps you are being asked to carry a particular burden for a season. Are you willing?

Can you accept it?
If the answer is 'no' to all of the above, this rock may be a particular boundary God has set for you personally, and you are no longer to challenge it. Can you let go and turn around to seek what God is doing that calls for your response?

Can you respect it?
Some stones are universal boundaries never to be crossed – biblical commandments and moral instruction, for example. These spiritual and ethical limits are to be heeded: in God's Kingdom the end does not justify the means.

---

reconfiguration restored her sense of vocation. With her vows as commitments of substance, not pledges of abstinence, she felt able to remain faithfully within her community. Hope was restored in a new 'inner freedom' and 'a renewed rootedness, an internal empowerment that was not there before'.[12]

Choosing to remain within our current circumstances at the end of our exploring is not necessarily a failure of nerve. It can take courage to live with greater authenticity and renewed vision within existing structures; to dare to face our inner disquiet and work through it to a place of acceptance. This is very different from trying simply to silence our midlife dissatisfaction by ignoring it until it goes away, and doggedly defending our current life.

Knowing we have chosen our course willingly, not resigned ourselves to it reluctantly, makes all the difference to our peace of mind and the quality of our life ahead.

Three biblical midlife women

One who left home . . .

Sarah left country and kindred with her husband Abraham in response to God's midlife call to possess a new land and found a nation. Her willingness to travel in trust alongside Abraham equalled his obedience, as she let go her settled existence for the unknown.

The fuller implications of this couple's journey unfolded as God spoke directly about the son to be born to them, the first of many descendants. Their destinies were caught up in God's long-term plans as their journey led them beyond their own resources, transforming and maturing their characters en route.

Their faith was tested as God's promise of a child and heir came to fruition 25 years after his call. Sarah's doubts that God's pledge of parenthood included her led to Abraham begetting Ishmael through her slave-girl, Hagar. Moreover by the time God announced that Isaac's conception was imminent, Sarah was post-menopausal. Yet God faithfully brought Sarah through the risks of a late pregnancy to give birth at his appointed time.

Do we dare respond to God's call to a new journey at midlife? Doing so can lead to unexpected new life being brought forth from within. Can we hear the whispered promise of an 'Isaac' to us?[13]

One who returned home . . .

Naomi's midlife journey was made in the aftermath of loss. She had come to Moab with her husband Elimelech and two sons to escape famine in Judah. Subsequently all three menfolk died. Naomi's sons left Moabite widows behind them.

Naomi's return to Judah was no triumphant homecoming but one of grief and emptiness. At midlife we can feel utterly alone. But Ruth, Naomi's daughter-in-law, softened her isolation by insisting on accompanying her. At midlife God does not leave us bereft but may provide some unexpected travelling companions. Will we accept them?

Naomi experienced bitterness at returning to her roots with apparently nothing to show for her life, yet God was already at work, transforming her second journey.

As Ruth gleaned corn, she found herself in the field of Boaz, a distant relative of Naomi's and a potential kinsman-redeemer. Sensing God's sovereign hand in her circumstances, Naomi encouraged Ruth to request Boaz's provision for her family's future. Her active response was rewarded when Boaz redeemed Elimelech's property and married Ruth. When the couple gave birth to Obed, the community declared: 'a son has been born to Naomi'.

Like Naomi, midlifers may experience God fashioning new patterns out of existing material: what seemed lost for good re-emerges via a different route. Naomi's hope and dignity were renewed, and her family line restored, as she nursed the child who would become King David's grandfather.[14]

One who stayed at home . . .

Lydia illustrates that a midlife journey does not necessarily mean a geographical shift. The little we know of this first-century woman from Philippi indicates that she was of significant rank. Lydia was the head of her household and thus probably widowed or single. She also flourished as a trader of the purple cloth renowned in her region. Yet she entered a new stage of life as she became Paul's first European convert. Her household followed on.

Lydia's second journey led her to offer hospitality to Paul and Silas: a well-established society woman welcoming the men at its margins. When Paul and Silas were dramatically imprisoned and divinely released, they went straight to Lydia's home, where other believers were already gathered. Her initiative and continuing example left a rich legacy: Paul's letter to the Philippian church highlights its warmth and practical, loving concern.[15]

Midlife may mean making space to include people and things once outside our parameters, as well as summoning the courage to embrace deeper values, regardless of our outer reputation.[16]

Reflecting and responding

1 Take time to work through the questions in the boxes in this chapter. What emerges? What changes do you need to make as a result?

2 Draw and colour a vine to represent your life just now. Which are the strong branches? Where is the fruit?

   Pray and ask God to show you how he wishes to tend and nurture the vine. Which branches need to be pruned, encouraged, fed and supported? Share this with a trusted friend and ask for their insights: remember that since fruit is primarily for others to enjoy, we may not be able to assess our own fruitfulness accurately.

3 How much are you engaged in the present moment? Choose a day to seek to stay tuned in to the 'here and now'. Engage your full attention and be gently persistent in being relaxed and receptive to what is around and within each moment. If possible, leave your watch at home and see it how feels not to have this point of reference with you. How does this change your experience of the day?

   If the above feels too demanding, choose one task as a focus. For example, use a walk or a journey that you make regularly. As you go, use all your senses to be attentive to your surroundings. What do you notice that you have previously just passed by without experiencing?

4 Break the mould! Try out a hobby, interest or activity that has always attracted you but you have never made time for. Rearrange a room, take a different route to an old place, try a new food etc. How does it feel to explore new possibilities?

8

Continuing the journey

—•◦•—

Reflections on life's road

Some people travel in straight lines:
Sat in metal boxes, eyes ahead,
Always mindful of their target,
Moving in obedience to coloured lights and white lines;
Mission accomplished at journey's end.

Some people travel round in circles:
Trudging in drudgery, eyes looking down,
Knowing only too well their daily, unchanging round,
Moving in response to clock and to habit;
Journey never finished, yet never begun.

I want to travel in patterns of God's making:
Walking in wonder, gazing all around,
Knowing my destiny, though not my destination,
Moving to the rhythm of the surging of His Spirit;
A Journey which when life ends, in Christ has just begun.

Julia McGuinness[1]

The real voyage lies not in seeking new landscapes, but in having new eyes.

Marcel Proust

What you and I become in the end will be just more and more of what we are deciding and trying to be right now.

John Powell

We are not permitted to choose the frame of our destiny. But what we put into it is ours.

Dag Hammarskjöld

You did not choose me, but I chose you. And I appointed you to go
and bear fruit, fruit that will last, so that the Father will give you whatever you ask him in my name.

John 15.16

Changing altitude

'We're going hill-climbing!' is the excited intention of many a visi-
tor to the Lake District. It brings to mind the promise of straining
limbs rewarded by spectacular views. Climbers focus on the effort of
ascent, looking ever upward towards their objective, finally achieving the summit and surveying the scene with a restful eye. The view
may live up to expectations or be disappointingly obscured by cloud
(not unknown in those parts!), but whatever the mountain-top
experience, moving on involves descent – there is nowhere else to
go.

This is the unanticipated part of the journey, for hill-climbers also
need to be hill-walkers, able to manage the distance downward as well
as up. Making the midlife transition is about turning into the journey's second phase, with its different demands and delights.

The descent is an integral part of a hill-walking expedition.
Warmed muscles are stretched again, fresh ones brought into play.
A different rhythm and quality of concentration are called for, a skil-
ful balance of control and letting go down the slope. Urgency to reach
the top gives way to a more measured pace. We can pause to savour
the changing view, our knowledge of what it looks like from higher
up bringing a new perspective on all we observe of the valley's activity below. And there is an assuredness in our step that derives from
knowing our direction: we are heading for home.

We have charted how the revolution of midlife upheaval can
bring the experience of isolation, and even exile, from a way of life
we thought was settled and sorted. The resolution of this upheaval is
marked by a growing sense of homecoming. More accommodating
of our whole selves, more authentic in our relationship with God and
more accepting of those around us, we come home to a life enriched
at every level.

As Macon Levy, a character in Anne Tyler's novel *The Accidental Tourist* remarks of his own midlife journey, 'I'm more like myself than I've been my whole life long.'[2]

Being 'over the hill' does not mean over and done with. Far from it. For those who engage with its choices and challenges, a new quality of being eventually emerges beyond the watershed of the midlife shift.

Studies made of artists' careers have shown that reaching the midlife point can herald a crisis. Those who survive with their vocation intact often come into a golden age of even greater creativity, as did the composer Johann Sebastian Bach. Yet their work may be qualitatively different, as the intense brilliance of the early years gives way to a more considered creativity. Compare, for example, the passionate intensity of Shakespeare's *Romeo and Juliet* with the more complex and courageous explorations of humanity in *King Lear*. The former was written as Shakespeare turned 30, the latter around a decade later.

But not everyone can use personal compositions, musical or dramatic, to chart the changing character of the second journey. It is ultimately in the art of everyday living that we must look for evidence of what it means to have negotiated the midlife divide effectively and emerged into a new stage.

Negotiating midlife transition is no quick fix. It may take some time and we need to be patient. As with adolescence, mid-olescence has its own unique unfolding course for different personalities and circumstances. Some describe a gradual turning over 3–5 years. For others it has been more like 7–9, or even a complete decade, before they can fully identify with a significant transformation. One reason it is hard to pinpoint progress is that this journey is more about learning a new way of travelling than about striving to reach a defined goal. It is like the difference between focusing on eating habits rather than weight; enjoying an occupation for its own sake rather than for material reward; paying attention to inner life rather than outer image; fostering a way of life rather than following a list of rules. The second journey is a way of being into which to grow more deeply, rather than a set of behaviours to be manufactured.

As we choose to face the challenges of midlife change, we will find that periods of disorientation and darkness are gradually permeated

---

Box 20   Conquest by circling

When Joshua led God's people into the Promised Land, occupying their inheritance entailed conquering the walled city of Jericho. God's battle strategy seemed strange: instead of rushing at the walls, the Israelites were to march round them daily in silence. On the seventh day, seven circlings would be followed by a long note on the priestly trumpets. As God's people shouted out in response, the walls would collapse, allowing them to enter the vanquished city.

At midlife, the constructions that need to fall may not yield to direct attack. We may have to walk alongside some old strongholds, instead of striving to obliterate them in our own strength; to take a more oblique path, trusting in God's power to bring victory at the right time.

The Israelites walked, worshipful and alert, behind the Ark of the Covenant that signified God's presence. Midlifers, too, need to focus on keeping in step with the spirit; to listen for the direction of the still small voice, and not use up energy trying to control or crush.

This can be hard. Jericho's inhabitants may well have felt amused contempt as they looked over their walls. And as we walk on past the enemies that mock our appearance of weak acceptance, we may wonder about the wisdom of our course.

At midlife we can feel we are going round in circles, with little dramatic change to show for our journey beyond a few more cracks in unyielding walls. But as we obediently re-tread the ground, the powers of the old ways are being shaken step by step, and will eventually fall. Our walk of faith is a valuable time of preparation, of building our inner resources to handle the exposure and vulnerability that the new space and freedom will bring.[3]

---

with times of inner certainty and clearer insight. Bit by bit a new sense of well-being and personal groundedness comes to undergird the ebb and flow of daily living.

As we accept this process of growth we can learn to lean into the rhythm of midlife transition: the time to be firm with ourselves and the time to be gentle; the time to act and the time to reflect; the time to hold on tenaciously and the time to let go totally.

We may find ourselves reworking old ground, feeling as though we are going fruitlessly round in circles, yet this can be a necessary prelude to breaking through to a new level of living (see Box 20).

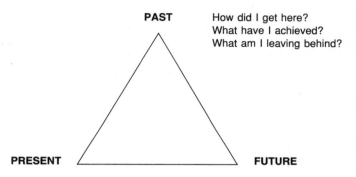

Figure 2 Midlife triangle of time

Tackling the triangle

Our exploration of midlife transition throughout this book has progressed through aspects of our past, present and future. But a key characteristic of this stage – at whatever age we experience it – is that it raises issues on all three fronts at once. The midlifer feels the squeeze in the middle. As one described it, 'Longings for the past collided with fears for the future, and the present lost its meaning.'

It is this unique combination of pressure-points that threatens to become a catalyst for crisis. These elements do not arise in the neat, ordered succession of a straight line. Indeed, we may feel them coming at us in a random and chaotic manner, but one way of summarizing them together is as a midlife triangle of time (see Figure 2).

Moving through midlife creatively means resolving the questions raised at each corner of the triangle. The psychotherapist Jane Polden describes the midlife task as to 'redeem the past, restructure the present, and refocus the future'.[4] We have considered this task throughout this book, but the core considerations can be summarized through a midlife triangle of engagement (see Figure 3).

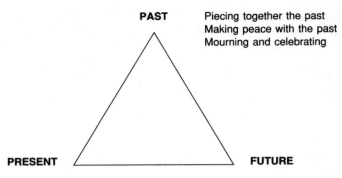

PAST — Piecing together the past
Making peace with the past
Mourning and celebrating

PRESENT
Attending to the inner life
Accepting and integrating the
whole self
Negotiating new ways of living

FUTURE
Preparing for ending
Identifying passion and
purpose
Setting future priorities

Figure 3 Midlife triangle of engagement

While these issues are generally characteristic of midlife transition, their individual timing, relevance and application to us will vary greatly. The midlife passage through to mature adulthood is a very personal one. Some corners of the triangle may feel particularly piercing; they may interconnect in different ways for different people; we may find ourselves very much focused on one aspect or moving backwards and forwards between two, or all three points.

But whatever our direction, disorientation and doubling back as we engage with issues that cry out to be addressed, the eternal triangle of the Trinity surrounds us and can indwell us.

The mysteriously interconnected life of Father, Son and Holy Spirit can contain and sustain us in our faith journey, soothing the sharp corners and reconciling us at every angle.

Reconnection

Moving creatively through midlife transition demands perseverance and trust, staying with the process and resisting the temptation to give up. An element of decision is involved for this change to be fruitful:

getting older is no guarantee of becoming wiser. As Gail Sheehy observes, 'Second adulthood is a career choice' involving 'the feeding and crafting of the soul.'[5]

Yet rising to the challenge to change is not so much a commitment to battle as a willingness to receive the opportunities for growth that emerge from within and around us in our midlife season. By listening and responding to whatever is unsettling our equilibrium, we allow the person we have become through our own making to be re-worked into the person we are created to be. We are choosing to move further along the path towards wholeness, a quality Margaret Guenther notes, writing on spirituality in life's second half, that is not 'the unblemished wholeness of the perfect newborn, but rather the worn wholeness that grows out of a lived life'.[6]

For those who hold to the midlife road, the struggle of transition ultimately gives way to the experience of transformation as these travellers on the second journey testify:

I have a sense of calmness and acceptance. I know who I am, and I'm comfortable with myself. It was a long, hard process getting here. It took about seven years of angst, followed by three years of increasing peace. When I came to the end of that journey I realized I'd reached the beginning of a new chapter. I'm looking forward to whatever the future holds, 'good' or 'bad'. I'm excited by the unknown. I'm not afraid of ageing or death any more. I'll live life to the full as long as I'm around.

I've appreciated my husband's support, I'm enjoying my children, and my relationship with my mother has changed. Nothing's actually been said, but somehow we've both realized I can no longer be manipulated by her as I once was. I've finally grown up.

Debbie

As a clergyman, the biggest transformation was being freed to be me – to explore and experiment, without feeling I had to impress people and get everything right all the time. It's a letting go that has been very relaxing.

I don't have to be in control. The work of ministry is not mine, it's God's, and he gives me a part in it. This freedom has given me a much more co-operative approach. I can allow and appreciate the contribution others make to God's work. I don't have to do and be it all.

John

I'm prepared to take more risks now because I know who I am and where my security lies. I'm able to be more tolerant and less judgemental. I can accept others' views more easily, and that people may be at different stages on different journeys.

I've learned I'm not perfect and that that's OK. There's the freedom of not having to set out to prove anything any more. I can move out into new waters and explore, and throw off some old restraints. I've also had years of proving God. He's led me thus far, and can take me on. I'm travelling with him, discovering new aspects of his character as I go. My second journey is an ongoing journey. I don't think I'll ever reach the end.

Anne

The above testimonies reflect some recurring themes in the experience of those who have come creatively through to the other side of midlife transition: sorrow at loss giving way to the joy of discovery; a striving for mastery replaced by a relaxation of control; rigidity of judgement yielding to greater acceptance and inclusiveness.

A deepening sense of personal identity undergirds all of these shifts. It provides the secure inner base that enables more outer room for manoeuvre. Yet each person's transition is as unique as it is typical. Your midlife story will share some common features with that of others, but the details of what you need to resolve will be yours alone. There are no set answers about what decisions to make as you engage with the issues that surface at midlife. The important thing is to engage positively with the process of resolving them (see Box 21).

The second journey, as Anne testified, is an ongoing journey. At midlife we face important decisions about how we will live, with all the benefits of experience and hindsight and all the potential to make some new choices. We will come to reap the consequences of those choices in days to come, just as we now have to reckon with the landscape that results from our decisions of early adulthood. As Erik

---

Box 21   Sailing the seven Cs of the second journey

Centred	Living according to inner integrity, not outer pressures
Connected	Loving others more yet needing them less
Calm	Trusting, with an attitude unruffled by life's uncertainties
Curious	Delighting in discovery, alive and attentive to the moment
Contemplative	Living at God's pace and making space for God
Courageous	Taking the risk of revealing one's true self, being vulnerable
Creative	Adaptable and accepting, able to work with whatever is to hand

---

Erikson observed in his work on the psychology of life-stages, 'The cornerstones for fruitful late life are set in middle years', whatever the timing and duration of the 'middle' and 'late' seasons in our particular life-course.[7]

Returning to the garden

For *Christine Mullins*, a married mother of five, moving through midlife meant both transition and crisis. She had responded to a midlife call to ministry, but just two months before being ordained, was diagnosed with pancreatic cancer and given six months to live. Christine was 45. As she observes, 'You live life without boundaries, and then all of a sudden, the walls close right in.'

Although tempted to withdraw from her curate's post, Christine was finally inspired to 'go for it', through a supportive message from a praying friend, who quoted the missionary Hudson Taylor: 'God's work in God's time never lacks God's resources.' Christine passed her six allotted months of life still working as a busy city-centre curate, alongside regular chemotherapy treatment that was continuing to contain the cancer.

Christine's faith became 'even more of a reality' as she came to terms with a foreshortened second half of life and the mystery of God's timing. She took comfort from Psalm 139, and reached an acceptance that 'God already knows all my days, including the timing of my ordination. Prayer has not given me any insight as to why things have turned out this way, but I believe God is in control.'

Christine's determination to make the most of her particular second journey has meant using every opportunity to treasure time with her family and fulfil her ministry. She has a deeper awareness of God's sustaining presence with her as she walks the road with cancer as a fellow-traveller. And she has sensed the closed-in walls drawing back: 'I feel well, and cancer is not preventing me from doing anything I want to do. It's as though I'm living in a walled garden. The boundaries are still there, but there's still space to move and grow things.'

The image of the walled garden resonates through Scripture as a picture of our relationship with our creator. At midlife it can re-emerge with particular power and poignancy. We see afresh the possibilities for new landscapes and greater fruitfulness, alongside the solidity of God's boundaries.

God planned for our life with him to grow in the garden as he planted and placed Adam and Eve within the Garden of Eden. Here they could express creativity and exercise dominion in harmony with God's sovereign will. Yet the human desire for independent rule led Adam and Eve to rebel against God's boundaries, and they were no longer at home there.

But God constantly calls his people back to life in the garden, and key scenes in the drama of humankind's redemption took place in garden settings. As God was betrayed in the Garden of Eden, so was his Son in the Garden of Gethsemane, his crucified body laid to rest in the closed-in walls of a garden tomb. But when Jesus rose from the dead and walked out of his grave to encounter Mary Magdalene in the garden, he restored it as a place of divine–human encounter.[8]

Israel under God's blessing is seen as a well-watered garden, nourished, ordered and fruitful.[9] The garden is a place for stillness and activity; for work and play; for the effort of planting and the grace of growth.

At midlife we may recognize our need for some personal garden restoration. The issues raised in this book have looked at how we may feel:

- claustrophobia, a feeling of walls closing in
- dismay at a vista of uncultivated wilderness
- dryness of the desert
- sorrow at what has been lost in our own personal Gethsemane
- alienation from the head gardener
- confusion at tangled growth
- uncertainty about how to cut through and bring all to order
- concern to ensure the fruitfulness of the plants that thrive most under our hands
- desire to create new landscapes
- frustration at the limited soil and space available
- excitement about discovering and uncovering hidden plants
- awareness of detail and design previously unnoticed

Whatever our situation at midlife, we can respond to God's call to cultivate what he has entrusted to us. The garden is the place where life with God begins and can begin again; where even what needs to be uprooted and burnt can be used to nourish new growth.

Midlife brings an inescapable awareness of God's walls around our life's garden. But it also brings a greater appreciation of the terrain within, in all its preciousness and potential. As we dig over the past, prune and prepare the ground in the present and plant for the future – ensuring we make channels for the flow of living water – we can approach our patch with renewed vision and vigour.

No two gardens are identical. A rich variety of landscape and design can be created; a distinctive array of shape, colour and kind of growth can be planted with the resources God has given. Almost infinite artistry can be expressed within finite walls. Midlife brings the creative adventure of discovering what we can do with what God has given, alongside the mature challenge of choosing what we shall do.

Gardening may be a solitary activity, just as midlife is a time for reflection, individual inner work and a sense of being alone. Yet this does not ultimately mean isolation. The walled garden can be a place of intimate meeting with the beloved, as the poet of the Song of Solomon celebrates. It is a special, personal place where we can be ourselves and deepen our relationship with the one who loves us most.[10]

When Mary Magdalene met the risen Christ in the garden, she mistook him for the gardener. Yet at midlife, Christ, who is the gardener and guardian of our souls, walks out to meet us afresh in the walled garden. As we welcome his unchanging presence in our changing times, we can regain the hope that the best season of life is yet to unfold.

Reflecting and responding

1 Take a walk, preferably up a hill, or somewhere where you have a clearly defined half-way point. Monitor your reactions and feelings on the journey. Does it make a difference when you know you are on your way home?

2 Visit a walled garden. First, walk around it, prayerfully. Ask God to speak to you through the plants, paths and landscapes that you see. What does this say to you about how he is at work in the garden of your life? What is he calling you to do to co-operate with him in tending this garden? Second, find a quiet corner or bench and imagine Christ coming towards you as the 'gardener' that Mary Magdalene encountered on the day of Resurrection. This is your private, special meeting with Christ. What do you most want to say that is for him alone to hear? How does he respond?

3 Look again at the seven Cs of the second journey (Box 21). Which of these reflects your experience? Are some more important to you than others? Which C do you most long for? Offer this to God in prayer as a potential point of personal growth. As you pray, make space to listen, to hear how you can respond to God to set sail into this C.

Midlife meeting ideas

Alongside individual reflection on the themes of this book, you might wish to set up a 'midlife group' for mutual support and further exploration of these issues. Below are some suggestions for shared activities, based on each chapter.

1 Charting the midlife landscape

Ice-breaker

Ask people to finish off the sentence:
'You know you've reached midlife when . . .'
This might trigger some brief discussion on whether midlife is an age or a stage.

Bible reading and discussion

Acts 2.17; 1 Corinthians 3.18–20

- From God's perspective, age is no bar to spiritual renewal. Compare and contrast this with your experience of the 'wisdom of this world' on ageing.
- How can we sustain a biblical outlook that affirms every life-stage amid the pressures and value judgements of a secular culture?

Psalm 107

- The psalm presents four dramatic pictures of God's people in troubled times: lost in the wilderness; imprisoned in darkness; weakened through illness; caught in a storm. Would any of these images describe the midlife crisis?
- What images would we suggest to encapsulate the midlife experience of crisis or transition?

Prayer activity
Journeying through life

You will need to collect and arrange a set of objects all connected with travelling. The selection can be as imaginative as you like – ticket, map, compass, AA membership card, timetable, brochure, walking boot, sunglasses, money, mobile phone, passport, pictures of road signs etc. Some gentle background music may also be useful for the reflection part of the exercise.

Explain that our life's journey takes us through different stages, times and seasons. We will start our prayer activity by listening and looking at the assembled objects, all concerning travelling. Ask the group to settle quietly and be open to the Spirit drawing their attention to whichever object underlines something about where they are on their life's journey right now.

After a period, invite people, if they wish, to share briefly what they have received. Then move this section into a time of praying for one another. You can ask people to pray brief, open spontaneous prayers if this is appropriate for the group. You may prefer to ask each person to pray for the one on their left, using a simple form of words such as: 'Lord, thank you for Sylvia/what Sylvia has shared. Please come alongside her on her journey.'

Draw this time to a close with a concluding prayer:

Thank you Lord, that though on life's journey we sometimes do not know the way to you, you always know the way to us.

And thank you for your promise that you are with us always, even to the end of the age. Amen.

2 *Making peace with our past*

Ice-breaker

Ask people to finish off the sentences:
'One of the best decisions I ever made was . . .'
'One of the worst decisions I ever made was . . .'
They should not think too long and hard over these, and some of the answers may well be light-hearted, as befits an ice-breaker.

Bible reading and discussion

Romans 8.28–30; Galatians 6.7–10; Proverbs 19.21

- Does God have one perfect path plotted out for us through life? If so, what happens if we take a wrong turning? If not, do we really need to seek his guidance in our decisions?
- How do we reconcile God's sovereignty with our choices as we reflect on our past?

Psalm 77.11–13; Philippians 3.13–17

- What would God have us remember and what are we to forget?
- How can we hold on to what we need to keep from the past, and let go of what we need to leave behind? Be practical.

Prayer activity

Giving thanks

You will need copies of the following prayer of the unknown Confederate soldier:

> I asked for strength that I might achieve.
> I was made weak that I might learn humbly to obey.
>
> I asked God for health that I might do greater things.
> I was given infirmity that I might do better things.
>
> I asked for riches that I might be happy.
> I was given poverty that I might be wise.
>
> I asked for power that I might have the praise of men.
> I was given weakness that I might feel the need of God.
>
> I asked for all things that I might enjoy life.
> I was given life that I might enjoy all things.
>
> I got nothing that I asked for –
> but everything I had hoped for . . .
>
> Almost despite myself, my unspoken prayers were answered.
> I am among all men most richly blessed.

Read the prayer together and ask people to reflect on it quietly. As they look back on their own lives, do they share the experience of having received different answers to their prayers and petitions? Are they aware of times when they have been given what they asked God for?

Have a time of open prayer, where you encourage people to speak out short prayers of thanksgiving for something that God has done in their lives, whether a desired or an unexpected blessing.

After each person prays, affirm their prayer by saying together a refrain from the Psalms, such as, 'Blessed be your glorious name for ever' or 'Thank you, Lord, for your steadfast love'.

Conclude by sharing God's Peace with one another.

3 Engaging with ageing

Ice-breaker

If you had the power to reverse one effect of ageing, which would you choose, and why?

Bible reading and discussion

1 Corinthians 9.24–27; Colossians 2.16, 17, 20–23; Proverbs 3.7, 8

- As Christians, how should we treat our bodies? How should our faith affect what we put in our bodies and what we do with them?
- How significant for you is the link between physical and spiritual health? Has your view on this changed in the light of your own experience?

Psalm 92; Proverbs 16.31

- Verses 12–15 in Psalm 92 highlight the longevity and fruitfulness of the faithful. Call to mind any senior Christians you know whom these verses could describe. What qualities about them do you admire?
- What do they teach us about how we need to live now, so that our own grey hair may be 'a crown of glory'?

Prayer activity

Offering our bodies

You may wish to have some suitable music playing as gentle backdrop to this activity.

Ask the group to assume a relaxed but alert posture, close their eyes, and become quietly conscious of their breathing, in and out. Read Romans 12.1–2:

> I appeal to you therefore, brothers and sisters, by the mercies of God, to present your bodies as a living sacrifice, holy and acceptable to God, which is your spiritual worship.

Explain that we are going to offer our bodies to God in prayer. As each part is named, a space will be left for silent response. This could be in stillness, or might include an individual movement (such as raising an arm) or gesture (such as placing a hand on part of the body) to express this self-giving.

> In him we live and move and have our being. And so we offer . . .
>
> Our head . . . our minds and all we think . . . our eyes, ears and all our senses . . . our mouths and all we say . . . (pause)
>
> Our shoulders and back, and all we carry . . . (pause)
>
> Our arms and all we do . . . our hands and all we touch . . . (pause)
>
> Our body's centre . . . our heart and all we feel . . . our lungs and all we breathe in . . . our vital organs and all that sustains our very life itself . . . (pause)
>
> Our deepest places and all that impassions us . . . Our vital organs and all our sexuality and nurturing energy . . . (pause)
>
> Our legs and all we stand for . . . our feet and all our walking . . . (pause)
>
> We offer to God any part that causes us particular discomfort, pain or concern, asking that he might touch that place and bring his wholeness . . . (pause)
>
> And finally we make space to listen for anything specific God's spirit wants to say to us about how he would have us express our spiritual worship through our bodies . . . (pause)

As Christians together, we form the united body of Christ, so we can conclude our prayers by joining in the Grace together:

[All] And the grace of our Lord, Jesus Christ, and the love of God, and the fellowship of the Holy Spirit be with us all, ever-more. Amen.

4 *Looking outside in*

Ice-breaker

Neither old nor young, midlifers could be pictured as part of the sandwich generation: 'Like a sandwich filling, midlifers may be less visible, but provide an essential element of nourishment in the middle.' (See pages 40.)

What sandwich filling best describes you?

Bible reading and discussion
1 Corinthians 9.19–23; Galatians 2.11–14

- Paul became 'all things to all people' yet took issue with Peter for changing his behaviour in response to those around him. To what extent should we personally accommodate others' expectations and sensitivities?
- How do we resolve the tensions between outer pressures and inner priorities?

Isaiah 40.3–5

- God's glory is seen in how he transforms the dry, hard and rough places. Where are our own midlife wildernesses and uneven ground – the places and people we would rather avoid?
- How can we 'prepare' these areas to receive God's presence? Have we any experience of God watering and levelling our own tough terrain?

Prayer activity
Known and loved

You will need to prepare pieces of paper with different Scripture verses written on them, such as those suggested below. It is best to have more

than enough for each person (you could use the same verse several times).
Spread these out in the middle of the group as you open the prayer time.
Suggested verses:

Jesus says 'As the Father has loved me, so I have loved you.' (John 15.9)

The Lord says 'I have chosen you . . . do not fear for I am with you.' (Isaiah 41.10)

The Lord says 'You are precious in my sight, and honoured, and I love you.' (Isaiah 43:4)

Jesus says 'I do not call you servants . . . I have called you friends.' (John 15.15)

I pray you may 'know the love of Christ that surpasses knowledge'. (Eph. 3.19)

I pray 'you may know what is the hope to which he has called you'. (Eph. 1.18)

Explain that in all we do as Christians, we can lose sight of who we are in Christ. We will pray for this knowledge of Christ's love to be renewed in one another.

Invite the group to be quiet and prayerfully reflect on the verses, be open to which one might be appropriate for the person on their right. When they sense a particular verse coming to their attention, they pick up that piece of paper and read it to the person, giving them the written verse afterwards. When all have read and received verses, close the prayer time by saying the Grace together, making sure that you look at one another as you do so.

5 Living inside out

Ice-breaker

Here's one you need to have prepared earlier! Give each person a numbered piece of paper on which you have written a short list comprising one half of a pair or opposites (Bonnie, cold etc.). Spread the other halves around different pieces of paper. The task is to find who has each other half on their list (Clyde, hot etc.). The first one to locate all their pairs or opposites is the winner.

Bible reading and discussion
Matthew 13.24–30; 2 Corinthians 6.14–18

- How do we feel about tolerating the tares as well as welcoming the wheat? How easy is it to be sure which is which?
- How can we reconcile the parable with Paul's injunction that we be a separate and pure people? Where appropriate, discuss the issues in the light of the complexity of real-life situations.

Galatians 6.1–5

- Discuss what it might mean to 'bear one another's burdens', but allow all to 'carry their own loads'.
- Are people aware of a need to do some midlife redistribution of loads and burdens? If so, how might they go about this?

Prayer activity

You will need some pieces of different coloured plasticine and some stones (preferably rough rather than smooth). You also need a small basin, a jug of water and a standing Cross. Arrange these on the table in the middle of the group.

Explain that the prayer activity will be based on the Serenity Prayer, as we bring to God those things that we are to accept and those things we are called to change – and ask his wisdom to know which is which.

Settle the group into quietness and read the Serenity Prayer:

God give me the serenity to accept things which cannot be changed;
Give me courage to change things which must be changed,
And the wisdom to distinguish one from the other.

Ask people to spend some moments listening for the Spirit to underline for them an issue, person or situation they are not only unable to change, but that they sense God is asking them to accept. When ready, they take a stone that represents what has come to mind, and place it in the basin as an act of willingness to accept it.

After everyone has done this, pour the water over the stones, with a short prayer inviting the Lord's living water to work on what is hard and immovable to us.

Then ask everyone to take a piece of plasticine, to represent an aspect of their life that they are called to change. Again ask people to listen for the Spirit to bring a particular aspect to mind, and to be open to what action he might be calling them to take. As they listen, they may wish to mould and work the plasticine in their hands, to express their willingness to respond in active obedience.

Ask people, when ready, to place the plasticine by the Cross, as an act of commitment to whatever they are being called to do. (They may wish to form the plasticine into a particular shape before doing so.)

Finally, pray a short prayer that God will empower people to fulfil their commitments. Close by reading Ephesians 3.20–21:

Now to him who by the power at work within us is able to accomplish abundantly more than we can ask or imagine, to him be glory in the church and in Christ Jesus to all generations, for ever and ever. Amen.

Note: The Serenity Prayer is the 1932 wording by Dr Reinhold Niebuhr.

6 Facing our mortality

Ice-breaker

What piece of music would you like to be played or sung at your funeral? What is special about it for you?

Bible reading and discussion
Matthew 6.34; 2 Peter 3.8–13

- How do we hold together living for today alongside waiting for 'the day of the Lord'?
- To what extent should we make earthly plans, given our heavenly destiny? Why invest in pensions and set long-term goals amid life's transience and uncertainty?

1 Corinthians 15.51–58

- Explore what impact these words concerning Christ's victory over death make in the light of our own ending.
- Discuss times in life that have brought a particular awareness of death's reality. What difference have these occasions made to people's outlook, faith or way of living?

Prayer activity

Living light

You will need one large, new white candle, plus a range of candles of varying shapes and sizes that have all been previously lit and burnt down to some degree. Arrange these centrally, with the white candle in the middle. You will also need one tea-light candle per person, and copies of the final prayer response. You may wish to use some appropriate gentle background music.

Start by lighting the white candle. Explain that this represents the light of Christ. The partly burnt candles represent our lives: mid-way through their course, yet still able to shine brightly with life. Ask everyone to choose a candle, and light it from the central white candle.

Allow some moments for people to look at their candle and consider how it speaks of their lives, with its light and warmth, its height and worn-ness.

Now read these verses:

> For it was you who formed my inward parts; you knit me together in my mother's womb.

> In your book were written all the days that were formed for me when none of them as yet existed. (Psalm 139.13, 16)

Allow some space for people to continue to gaze at their candle and reflect on God's word in his presence.

Now read this verse:

> So teach us to count our days that we may gain a wise heart. (Psalm 90.12)

Allow people time to listen for the particular wisdom the Spirit would apply to their hearts at this time, in the light of the candle flame.

Now ask people to take a tea-light and light it from their candle, either setting it next to the candle or holding it. This is a reminder that in Christ, death has been conquered, and we have been given eternal life with him.

After some moments, conclude with the following words and response:

> Jesus says, 'I am the resurrection and the life. Those who believe in me, even though they die, will live, and everyone who lives and believes in me will never die.' Do you believe this?
>
> [All] Yes, Lord. We believe that you are the Messiah, the Son of God. Amen. (John 11.25–27)

7 Renewing our hope

Ice-breaker

Do you have a secret, burning ambition? What, given no outer constraints of circumstances, time, money etc. do you really dream of being or doing?

Bible reading and discussion
Jeremiah 1.4–19; Exodus 3.1–15; 4.1–5

- Jeremiah received God's call in youth, Moses in later life: compare the nature of their calls and their responses. When in our lives have we felt a new sense of call and purpose?
- How can we find our way forward when there seems to be no direct divine word or burning bush for us?

John 11.17, 38–44

- Consider Lazarus' story as a parable of midlife transition (you may want to look at the whole narrative from John 11:1 onwards). What parallels do we identify with?
- Discuss what might characterize the resurrected Lazarus' second adulthood?

Prayer activity

Setting our direction

You will need a clock and a compass to place in the middle of the group, and a candle. Start by placing the clock in the middle of a central table. You might wish to invite people to take off their watches and place them on the table in front of them too.

Explain that we live much of our lives measuring our activities by the clock. The first part of our prayer will be to let go of these activities into God's hands, trusting them to him, and releasing our sense of urgency and anxiety about the things we have to get done.

Open the prayer time with thanksgiving:

Lord, we praise you that you are Lord of all that has been, all that is, and all that is to come. Living God and Everlasting King, we thank you that our times are in your hands.

Invite people to surrender their activities and concerns to God with words such as:

Living God and Everlasting King, I offer to you my . . . (work, family tasks etc.).

Conclude this section of the prayer with the same words as before:

Lord, we praise you that you are Lord of all that has been, all that is, and all that is to come. Living God and Everlasting King, we thank you that our times are in your hands. Amen.

Now place the compass on the table and use it to find north. When you have done so, take the candle and place it outside the group and away from the table in the direction of north. Light the candle and ask the group to turn towards it.

Explain that in this section of the prayer time we will ask to receive the light of Christ and the fruit of the Spirit, that we might always express and grow into his likeness and closer to him through whatever we do.

Open this section of the prayer time with words such as:

Lord Jesus, we praise you that you are the light of the world.
Fill us with your life and light, we pray.

Invite people in the group to pray for more of Jesus in all that they
do, with words such as:

Lord Jesus, light of the world, please fill me with your . . .
(gentleness, wisdom, courage, love etc.).

Finish with much the same words as before:

Lord Jesus, we praise you that you are the light of the world.
Thank you that you delight to fill us with your light as we open
our lives to you. Amen.

8 *Continuing the journey*

Ice-breaker

What is it like to come home after a time away?

Bible reading and discussion

Philippians 2.12, 13; Ephesians 2.8, 9; James 2.18–23

- How do we understand the relationship between God's grace and
  our works in our daily lives?
- If a midlife reappraisal of our faith's activity versus receptivity means
  we want to make some changes, how can we shift the balance-point
  between the two? Be practical.

Micah 6.8

- How do we respond to this verse? Does Micah's simplicity denote
  wise maturity or naïve idealism? Can we make too much of midlife transition, or are we in danger of denying its complexities?
- Is there a difference between resignation and acceptance, or do
  both imply passivity and defeat? Where do you draw the line at
  midlife?

Prayer activity

Enfolded and protected

You will need to prepare a set of cut-out triangle shapes from coloured card, one for each person. You will also need pens for everyone and a standing Cross.

Explain that our journey through midlife raises issues around all three aspects of past, present and future, represented by the triangle figure. Though we may see this shape as pushing in on us from all three directions, the three sides also represent how Christ totally enfolds us and has each corner covered: Christ has died, dealing with our past; Christ is risen and alongside us in our present; Christ will come again, holding our future destiny in his hands.

Since this is the last gathering, invite each person to write a short prayer of thanksgiving on their triangle for something that they will take away with them (or perhaps a prayer of commitment for the next stage of their journey).

For the prayer time, group members take it in turns to read out their prayer, and place their triangle in front of the Cross. Encourage people to lay the triangles against one another so that they interlock, to express the fact that we are part of one body.

After each person's prayer, everyone declares:

Christ has died. Christ is risen. Christ will come again.

Conclude with the Grace as a way of affirming unity and mutual support as we part.

(You could also develop this idea using the three persons of the Trinity: God the Father, Creator of all from the very beginning; God the Son, alongside us where we are right now; God the Holy Spirit, giving us strength and hope for the future.)

Notes

1 Charting the midlife landscape

1 Gail Sheehy, *New Passages: Mapping your life across time.* HarperCollins, 1996.
2 Carl Jung, *Modern Man in Search of a Soul.* Routledge Classics, 2001.
3 2 Samuel 11—12.25.
4 1 Kings 19.1–18.
5 Job 42.

2 Making peace with our past

1 Luke 8.43–48; Mark 10.46–52; John 3.1–16.
2 Luke 24.13–35.
3 Elisabeth Kübler-Ross, *On Death and Dying.* Simon & Schuster, 1997.
4 Genesis 37—45.
5 Philippians 3.4b–11; Acts 9.1–30.

3 Engaging with ageing

1 C. Colarusso and R. Nemiroff, *Adult Development: A New Dimension in Psychodynamic Theory and Practice.* Plenum Press, 1981.
2 Gail Sheehy, *New Passages: Mapping your life across time.* HarperCollins, 1996.
3 Michael Jacobs, *The Presenting Past* (second edition). Open University Press, 1998.
4 1 Samuel 16.1–13.
5 Deuteronomy 14.22–27; John 21.4–14.
6 1 Corinthians 6.19–20.
7 Romans 12.1.
8 For Liz Babbs' story of recovery from ME and insights into the illness, see *Can God Help ME.* Authentic, 2005. See also her practical introduction to meditative prayer for active Christians, *Into God's Presence.* Zondervan, 2005.
9 Some helpful ways into stillness can be found in Anthony de Mello, *Sadhana: A Way to God.* Bantam Doubleday Dell, 1984.

4 Looking outside in

1 Poem used by kind permission of the author. Copyright Sue Mayfield.
2 Carl Jung (trans. R. F. C. Hull), *Two Essays on Analytical Psychology. The Collected Works of C. J. Jung, Vol. 7* (second edition). Princeton University Press, 1972.
3 Daniel 4.
4 Johari window. The Johari window is named after the first two elements of its creators' names. Joe Luft and Harry Ingham researched human personality at the University of California in the 1950s. The model focuses on how personality is expressed, and can be used to increase personal and interpersonal awareness.
5 The MBTI is an accessible, Jungian-based model that helps clarify personality profile. It emphasizes the value of all personalities, and offers helpful insights into many areas of life, including spirituality. The Retreat Association publishes an annual programme of retreat house events, including MBTI Workshops. Tel: 0845 456 1429. Website: www.retreats.org.uk
6 Philippians 2.12, 13.
7 For a practical, biblical approach to personal dreamwork, see Russ Parker, *Healing Dreams*. Triangle, 1993.

5 Living inside out

1 Glyn Brangwyn's poem was first published in Ray Simpson, *Exploring Celtic Spirituality*. Hodder & Stoughton, 1995.
2 1 Kings 12.1–19.
3 Joshua 1.1–5; 2 Samuel 12.13–15; John 21.15–19; John 8.3–11.
4 Daniel Levinson, *Seasons of a Man's Life*. Ballantine, 1986.
5 Genesis 32.22–32.
6 Luke 18.17.

6 Facing our mortality

1 William Raeper. Bill's varied writing also included: *The Troll, the Butterfly and Other Stories*. André Deutsch, 1987; *George MacDonald*. Lion Hudson, 1988; *A Beginner's Guide to Ideas*. Lion Hudson, 1991.
2 Elliott Jaques, 'Death and the Mid-life Crisis'. *International Journal of Psychoanalysis*, 46 (4): 502–14, 1965.
3 Margaret Guenther, *Towards Holy Ground*. Cowley Publications, 1995.

4 2 Timothy 4.6–8.
5 Psalm 139.16.
6 Romans 8.28.
7 Christianne Heal's comments are in the Natural Death Centre's *Natural Death Handbook*. Rider, 2003 (a sensitive and practical resource offering information on all aspects of death and dying).
8 David Watson, *Fear no Evil*. Hodder & Stoughton, 1984.
9 Advice in the *Natural Death Handbook* could be useful for this exercise.

7 Renewing our hope

1 Derek Milne, *Coping with a Mid-Life Crisis*. Sheldon Press, 2004.
2 George Vaillant, *Adaptation to Life*. Little, Brown, 1990.
3 William Bridges, *Transitions: Making Sense of Life's Changes*. Da Capo Press, 2004.
4 John 11.38–53.
5 Genesis 19.25–26.
6 Ephesians 2.10.
7 Bridges, *Transitions*.
8 D. B. Bromley, *Human Ageing*. Penguin, 1988.
9 Murray Stein, *In Mid-Life: A Jungian Perspective*. Spring Publications, 1983.
10 Psalm 16.5, 6.
11 Romans 12.2.
12 Joyce Rupp, *Dear Heart, Come Home*. Crossroad Publishing, 1996.
13 Genesis 12.1–5; 15.1–6; 16.1–6; 17.15–22; 18.1–15; 21.1–7.
14 Ruth 1—4.
15 Philippians 1.3–5; 4.15.
16 Acts 16.14, 15, 40; 17.4.

8 Continuing the journey

1 Copyright Julia McGuinness, previously published in Ian Bradley, *Colonies of Heaven: Celtic Models for Today's Church*. Darton, Longman and Todd, 2000; and in Peter Millar and Neil Paynter, *Our Hearts Still Sing*. Wild Goose Publications, 2004, www.ionabooks.com
2 Anne Tyler, *The Accidental Tourist*. Vintage, 1995.
3 Joshua 6.

Notes

4 Jane Polden, *Regeneration: Journey through the Mid-life Crisis.* Continuum, 2002.

5 Gail Sheehy, *New Passages: Mapping your life across time.* HarperCollins, 1996.

6 Margaret Guenther, *Towards Holy Ground.* Cowley Publications, 1995.

7 Erik Erikson, *Childhood and Society.* Vintage, 1995.

8 Genesis 3.1–13; Mark 14.32–50; John 20.11–18.

9 Isaiah 58.11; Jeremiah 31.12.

10 Song of Solomon 6.2, 3.

The Society for Promoting Christian Knowledge (SPCK) was founded in 1698. Its mission statement is:

To promote Christian knowledge by

- **Communicating the Christian faith in its rich diversity;**
- **Helping people to understand the Christian faith and to develop their personal faith; and**
- **Equipping Christians for mission and ministry.**

SPCK Worldwide serves the Church through Christian literature and communication projects in over 100 countries, and provides books for those training for ministry in many parts of the developing world. This worldwide service depends upon the generosity of others and all gifts are spent wholly on ministry programmes, without deductions.

SPCK Bookshops support the life of the Christian community by making available a full range of Christian literature and other resources, providing support for those training for ministry, and assisting bookstalls and book agents throughout the UK.

SPCK Publishing produces Christian books and resources, covering a wide range of inspirational, pastoral, practical and academic subjects. Authors are drawn from many different Christian traditions, and publications aim to meet the needs of a wide variety of readers in the UK and throughout the world.

The Society does not necessarily endorse the individual views contained in its publications, but hopes they stimulate readers to think about and further develop their Christian faith.

For further information about the Society, visit our website at *www.spck.org.uk* or write to:
SPCK, 36 Causton Street,
London SW1P 4ST, United Kingdom.